PAUL WILDER
MY QUEST FOR TV FAME

Written with Paul Burton

Foreword by Derek Martin

To Ruth
Smile and Have Fun!

Paul

x x

PAUL WILDER

MY QUEST FOR TV FAME

SMP Publishers

First published in 2009 by
SMP Publishers
Devonshire House
Manor Way
Borehamwood
Hertfordshire
WD6 1QQ
United Kingdom
Telephone: (0208) 736 0949

Email: smppublishers@aol.com
www.smppublishers.co.uk

All photographs printed within this book
are from Paul Wilder's private collection

Photographs of Jean-Christophe Novelli taken by Henry Velleman

A CIP catalogue record for this book is available
from the British Library

ISBN 978-0-9562842-0-4

Typeset by Whoosh Design (www.whooshdesign.co.uk)

Cover design: Mandy Lampard

Cover photograph Scott Kleinhesselink (www.scottkphoto.com)

Printed and bound in Great Britain by imprintdigital.net

SMP Publishers have made every effort to ensure that papers used
are natural, recyclable products made from wood grown
in sustainable forests. The manufacturing processes conform
to the environmental regulations of the country of origin.

This book is dedicated to my darling wife Suzanne, my beautiful daughter Melody, and my parents without whom ...

Paul Wilder

Never strive for fame, strive for a passion.

Jodie Prenger
(winner of BBC1's *I'd Do Anything*)

PAUL WILDER

MY QUEST FOR TV FAME

Contents

Foreword

My Mum was a big film fan and used to take me to the cinema three times a week from the age of about four and a half. She used to tell me to respect film, and my love for cinema really came from that.

I did my National Service and had many jobs including: rag and bone man, professional gambler, and I worked at Smithfield Meat Market where I got myself into a bit of trouble over £10,000 worth of meat, which was a lot of money in those days. Ending up at the Old Bailey I acted my socks off and got off the charge. It was after the court case that I wanted to be an actor. I didn't know where to start but I heard that a lot of actors hung about in coffee shops in Wardour Street and Old Compton Street. I got myself suited and booted and headed down to the coffee shop called, I think, Act 1 or Scene 1. I was aged twenty-nine.

I asked the actors who hung out there who their agent was and was given the telephone number of Terry Denton De Gray, an extras agent. After phoning Terry I was told to get myself down to the BBC, Wood Lane for three days on *Z Cars* as a walk on. It was filmed live and I was paid 3 guineas. ITV shows paid 4 guineas.

After that I really caught the bug and more extras work followed on shows like *Dixon of Dock Green*, *Adam Adamant* and *The Morecambe & Wise Show*. As well as working as an extra I joined Derek Ware's Stunt Agency and got hired as a stuntman. This went well until I broke my collar bone while working on *Elizabeth R*. This was around 1970. Following this I found an acting agent called Jimmy Garrett who remained with me for nineteen years.

My real big break came when I got a lead part of a bent copper in a controversial series called *Law and Order*. It was even discussed in Parliament at the time.

So my advice to Paul, or anyone else who wants to work in this industry either in front or behind the camera, is 'keep going, always be on time and be professional'. I never trained as an actor and I have never done theatre. I consider myself to be the luckiest man in showbiz.

I wish Paul Wilder the very best of luck with this book and all who sail in her!

Derek Martin
(Charlie Slater, *EastEnders*)
www.derekmartin.net

Introduction (by Paul Burton)

Paul Wilder always had it firmly fixed in his mind that he wanted to be on TV, but realised that he didn't have any specific talent. By his own admission he couldn't sing, couldn't play an instrument and, as far as he knew, couldn't act. But once Paul began to find ways of getting to appear on TV, his quest for continued TV fame really began in earnest.

I first became aware of Paul Wilder whilst watching an edition of the Big Brother *spin-off programme* Big Brother's Big Mouth. *This was back in the days when a certain comedian called Russell Brand (I wonder whatever happened to him?) was hosting the show with such enthused eloquence.*

For those of you who have never seen Big Brother's Big Mouth, *the premise is that the audience offers to the presenter/s their opinions on all things* Big Brother-*related including the current housemates.*

On one particular night that my bleary eyes were attempting to focus on the programme, late one night, Brand suddenly stuck his Terry Wogan/Blankety Blank-esque microphone under the mouth of a guy who turned out to be the hero of this book – Paul Wilder. Wilder instantly took charge, looking completely at home on set and delivering his opinions with the experience and panache that would have put some professional modern day television presenters to shame (I shall mention no names!). Here was a man who was almost holding court in the studio. It was obvious to me even then, when I knew nothing about his past TV experiences, that Paul was not only a passionate fan of all things Big Brother-*related, but a man who had obviously been in front of a television camera before. How little did I realise way back then just how at home he was in a television studio or, indeed, just how experienced he was in the world of television. Paul was a man who I was, in time, to discover had a quest and a passion for TV fame and a desire to be more than just a talking head as part of an audience on a television discussion show.*

We fast forward some two years and Wilder and I become acquainted due to our mutual enjoyable task of documenting all the latest events in the Big Brother *house during* Big Brother 9 *for our respective blogs on the website of the* Borehamwood & Elstree Times *newspaper. The aforementioned newspaper publication is, incidentally, delivered to residents who live in-and-around Elstree Studios in Borehamwood, where* Big Brother *is made. Knowing about my previous books, Paul asked at the start of 2009 if I would help to create his autobiography. Not wanting to ghost write his life story in the conventional way, I agreed to Paul's request on the condition that I write the book not as a ghost writer but as a kind of a tour guide through Paul Wilder's life; stopping off to allow the man himself to tell his own story recorded through a series of taped interviews at his Elstree home. And so that was what Paul and I agreed and the following book you are about to read takes the form of which I have just described. This way I feel you will get the real essence of Paul Wilder – TV extra, quiz show contestant, talking head, marathon runner and an all-round enthusiast who has a zest and a love for life and, most importantly, his family.*

I would personally like to thank three people whose patience and support was a God-send while I was writing this book. They are: Paul Wilder, himself, who invited me into his world to write this book for him and has always been ever-ready with a supply of time, recollections and enthusiasm. Secondly his wife, Suzanne Wilder, a very charming woman who was patient enough to allow me to spend endless hours in her dining room interviewing her partner on tape. Finally, I would like to thank their lovely daughter, Melody Wilder, who allowed me to use her father-related thoughts and recollections within this book.

I would also like to take this opportunity to thank, on behalf of both Paul Wilder and myself, actor Derek Martin for writing the foreword for this book and TV presenter Kaye Adams and comedian Leigh Francis for their respective words of encouragement and support with this project. We would also like to thank Paul's friends: Andy Cooper, Scott Kleinhesselink and Lorraine Silver for their respective Wilder-related recollections.

In the short time I have been lucky to know Paul and Suzanne I couldn't help but come to the conclusion that they are a perfect example to any would-be couples out there. Their support for each other, especially Suzanne's of Paul's on-going quest for TV fame, proves that couples can still achieve their individual dreams and aspirations without affecting their relationship.

So prepare to start a unique journey – a journey of the book variety – into the world of Paul Wilder as he recalls the ups and downs of his quest for TV fame.

Paul Burton
Writer, Filmmaker and Film & TV Historian
www.paulburton.org.uk
May 2009

Introduction (by Paul Wilder)

The American artist Andy Warhol once famously said in the late 1960s that: 'In the future, everyone will be world-famous for fifteen minutes'. It has also been said, although it's hard to know who to attribute the following quote to, 'That everyone has a book inside them'. Well, by the end of 2008 I myself was starting to think about the book that might be inside of me. I knew that I wanted to write a book, a book that was more than just a biography, but a book that would prove a must-read for anyone who is interested in the world of television and the fickle world of 'Celebrity'.

I love television and like millions of other people across the globe I watch hours and hours of TV a week. I enjoy viewing continuing dramas such as *The Bill*, *EastEnders* and *Holby City*. But my love of British TV programmes doesn't just stop there as I also embrace programmes as varied as *Never Mind the Buzzcocks*, *Celebrity Juice* and the gritty Channel 4 drama, *Shameless*.

I started appearing as a background artist in 2006 on some of the programmes that I have both watched and loved each week. For me, it was like dying and going to TV heaven! Taking part in TV debate shows like E4's *Big Brother's Big Mouth* and ITV2's *I'm a Celebrity Get Me Out of Here … Now!* has also added another string to my bow. Not forgetting a chance to air my own personal views on the TV shows they act as a spin-off for.

I first mentioned my proposed book idea to Paul Burton in passing at the end of 2008, but it wasn't until after the final night of *I'm a Celebrity Get Me Out of Here ... Now!* that I decided to make the idea a reality.

After the final edition of the show I started to chat to the host of the show Mark Durden-Smith, and he asked me what I planned to do next. I said probably a bit of *Celebrity Big Brother's Big Mouth* and hopefully more film and TV extra work.

On my way home from The London Studios, which is situated on London's South Bank and is where *I'm a Celebrity Get Me Out of Here ... Now!* is made, I thought about my chat to Mark and what I had said. Maybe, I thought, now is the right time to do more than make fleeting appearances on *Big Brother's Big Mouth* and be engaged in film and TV extra work. Maybe now is the time to get to work on a light-hearted book which features the various ups and downs that I have experienced during my long quest for TV fame.

In January 2009 I once again mentioned my book idea to Paul Burton and sent him three pages of ideas for the book. Paul thought that my book ideas would make an entertaining, informative and hopefully an inspiring publication.

So now there is no going back! It's time to share my adventures with the world and to prove that anyone can appear on his or her favourite TV shows. At the very least, I hope this book will inspire its readers to go and pursue their own ambitions.

I am not a trained actor, but I have now appeared in many TV shows and I am now a proud member of Equity. Equally, I am not a trained TV Presenter, but I have now appeared on many TV Quiz and Game Shows. Neither am I a trained writer, but I have now had my own book published and in the process been inspired to start a new publishing business. You see – dreams can come true!

I hope you enjoy reading my story, the ups and downs, the hopes and dreams and the two bans that have made up *My Quest for TV Fame*.

Paul Wilder
www.paulwilder.biz
May 2009

Chapter One
Bolan, Panto & Waffles

Paul B: The year 1972 had its fair share of ups and downs. Briton's reached for a set of candles on more than one occasion due to a miners' strike and cinemagoers flocked to their local cinema (if they still had one!) to watch (as and when power cuts allowed) Marlon Brando *appearing in* The Godfather. *Meanwhile, a certain Captain Peacock asked Mr Humphries: 'Are you free?' for the first time in the classic BBC TV sitcom,* Are You Being Served?

Younger reader's of this book may find it hard to comprehend, living as we all now do in this multi-channel age, that back in 1972 there were just three terrestrial TV channels available to watch in the UK. Back then, with no MTV to watch, Top of the Pops *was a must-see TV programme for all fans of the likes of David Bowie, Donny Osmond and Slade. And the hero of our story, Paul Wilder, was as much a fan as any of BBC1's* Top of the Pops. *Speaking to me over a hot cup of coffee in the dining room of his home in Elstree, Hertfordshire, he recalled:*

Paul W: My Musical leaning has always been to pop/rock. I had been to my first rock concert in 1971

1

to see Status Quo at the Marquee Club in Wardour Street, Soho. This blew me away.

Many live gigs followed including the opening night at the Sundown Club in Mile End Road where Slade blew the roof off!

The LP (Long Playing vinyl record disc) that was never off my turntable in the summer of 1972 was David Bowie's timeless classic: *The Rise and Fall of Ziggy Stardust* and the *Spiders from Mars*. Every track was brilliant. *Starman* is still one of my most favourite singles of all time, as is the Bowie penned *All the Young Dudes*, which Mott the Hoople took to No. 3 in the charts in 1972.

One of the most memorable gigs that I ever went to was at the Hammersmith Odeon in December 1973. This is where I saw the legendary Queen supporting Mott the Hoople. After which, I spent many an hour singing into a hairbrush in front of a mirror pretending to be a rock star, usually Ian Hunter (Mott's lead singer) or Marc Bolan of T.Rex.

I never made any secret of the fact that I always wanted to be a member of the audience on the *Top of the Pops* show but in those days it was just impossible to get a ticket – they were like gold dust! However, one day my friend Melvyn phoned me and said that his girlfriend, Jacqui (who was later to become his wife), had managed to get four tickets and they, along with another friend, Janis, were going to see a recording of the show on Wednesday 22nd November 1972. Melvyn then asked if I would be interested in going along to the show with them. Would I? Being such a huge fan of the programme I, of course, immediately said 'Yes'.

In those days I was the only one out of the four of us who could drive so, excitedly, I drove the four of us to BBC Television Centre in West London, where the show was taped in those days. Ironically, *Top of the Pops* would later move and be recorded at BBC Elstree in Borehamwood, just down the road from where I now live.

The show was recorded weekly on Wednesday nights and it was broadcast the following evening. When we arrived on this particular Wednesday in 1972, despite having tickets, we had to queue for a very long time outside the BBC Television Centre in the freezing cold before we were allowed in.

When we eventually entered the imposing studios – my first time in a TV studio – I could not believe that I was actually there with the *Top of the Pops* logo looking down on me.

The programme-makers warned us that that we were going to be constantly moved from one part of the studio to another very quickly. I remember that they were quite strict and it did feel as though we were part of some kind of cattle auction but I didn't mind – I was going to be on *Top of the Pops* and on BBC1! And this was in the days of the show's huge ratings!

Future *Deal or No Deal* presenter Noel Edmonds was hosting the show that week. I can remember pushing myself forward so that I could become one of the many grinning faces that were seen standing behind the host of the show each week. I had very long dark hair in those days and I was wearing a long mauve sleeve top with black stars on, oh, and tight loons. Everybody thought I was a hippy back then, I just loved the hippy fashions.

After the actual show had been recorded a member of the production team announced that they would be recording a video insert of a band playing in the studios for the following week's show. And who was the band in question? Well, none other than T.Rex who performed their then new song, *Solid Gold Easy Action*. I was in heaven! T.Rex gave out limited edition t-shirts with the words 'Solid Gold Easy Action' on them displayed in gold glitter writing on a black background. I wasn't happy some years later when my wife Suzanne threw mine out! I still remind her of that to this day!

Even these days I can recall that while T.Rex were performing in the studios I managed to push myself forward to the front of the crowd so that I could touch one of Marc Bolan's feet! I know it sounds stupid now but Bolan was one of my biggest heroes.

Paul B: Given that Paul had been one of Bolan's biggest fans, I asked him how he felt when the news was announced that the T.Rex singer had been tragically killed in a car crash (his girlfriend, Gloria Jones, survived the accident) on the 16th September 1977:

Paul W: I was devastated. I was even more upset about Marc's death than when Elvis Presley died just one month previously on 16th August 1977. I loved him and his lyrics. In fact I loved his whole image and showmanship.

Going back to *TOTP*, Chuck Berry was No. 1 in the charts that week with *My Ding-a-Ling* the week that we went to see the show being recorded.

I can clearly remember that there were several close-ups of the four of us in my group dancing together in the studio because the next day everyone was saying they had spotted us on TV! I also recall that when I watched the show being broadcast on the Thursday night I could clearly be seen standing behind Noel grinning like a Cheshire cat. So nothing has changed all these years later – I can still be spotted on TV shows doing the same kind of thing! But this was the first time I had appeared on TV and unbeknown to me a spark had been lit that would ultimately set me on my way on my quest for TV fame. However, despite my small brush with TV fame it would be seventeen years before I would appear on my next TV show (the game show *Every Second Counts*) and return to the BBC Television Centre.

I've always watched the Steve Wright-hosted television show *TOTP2* in the hope of seeing a clip of us on the edition we appeared on back in 1972, but I have had no luck as yet.

Paul B: Since we first spoke about Paul's visit to Top of the Pops, *he emailed to inform me that he had spotted a clip of himself and one of his friends dancing along to T.Rex on* Top of the Pops *uploaded on to the internet video website,* YouTube.

But long before the first initial spark of inspiration was fired up by Paul's appearance on Top of the Pops *that would in-time see Paul begin a full blown quest for TV fame, came, of course, his big entrance into the world.*

* * *

Paul W: I was born at 7.30 am on Saturday 5th March 1955 at Kingsbury Maternity Hospital in Honeypot Lane, London, NW9. It was a very cold morning but the sun was shining.

By tradition, my first name had to be taken from a late relative. My father decided that he wanted to choose the name of my late grandfather on my dad's side of the family. The English version of which was Leon, and my name would go on to be registered as Leon Paul Wilder. However, my mother didn't like the name Leon and wanted my first name to be Paul. So, by way of a compromise, my name was registered as Leon Paul Wilder, but I would henceforth be known as simply Paul Wilder.

After I was born I became seriously ill. In fact I still have the scar some 54 years later to prove it. My food tubes became blocked up and the doctors told my parents that I had Pyloric Stenosis, and so I was rushed to Great Ormond Street Children's Hospital in London.

My mum was also unwell and taken into Wembley Hospital where she was treated for deep vein thrombosis and pleurisy. My dad did not tell her at the time that I had been admitted to Great Ormond Street. He had to dash backwards and forwards between us both. Fortunately, I recovered after about six weeks but it was touch and go as to whether I would survive. My parents were told at the time not to have any more children; but they obviously didn't take the doctors' advice as they went on to give me two brothers: Simon and Martin.

We lived at Farrer Road in Kenton, Middlesex, off the Kenton Road until I was about 10 years old and then moving not far away to Shaftesbury Avenue in Kenton.

Initially, I went to Glebe Primary School in Kenton after the move, and I later went to what was, at the time, called Claremont Comprehensive School in Claremont Avenue off the Kenton Road. When it came to the Eleven Plus I was told that I was a 'border line case' (I didn't like the sound of that – and still don't!) and, sadly, this 'border line case' didn't quite make it into Grammar School.

Paul B: Noting a flicker of irritation as he recalled his failure to negotiate his way into Grammar School, I asked Paul whether this was something that he ended up regretting:

Paul W: No, not really. I ended up with a lot of good friends who I met through the local youth club.

Paul B: Given Paul's long-running obsession for TV fame, I then asked whether he considered himself to have been an outgoing child:

Paul W: No, I was a very shy child and pretty average at school. I think my parents are still quite amazed even now when they see me taking part in all these debate shows like *Big Brother's Big Mouth* and *I'm A Celebrity Get Me Out of Here … Now!* Because, up until a certain age, I wouldn't even have said boo to a goose! But somewhere along the line something must have changed within me because I became a lot more extrovert.

Despite my shyness at school, I do, however, recall appearing in two school plays. I was cast in a play at Glebe, although I didn't have a lead role or anything. I can't remember what the play was called but I can remember that I played the part of a ragamuffin and that they dressed me in rags and put grease paint on my face to make me look dirty. I had just one line which I can still remember to this day: 'I have some apples for you'.

The other school play I was cast in saw me playing the narrator and that for me, at the time, was quite nerve-racking. I recall that I had to come on to the stage and that the curtains closed behind me as I entered. I then had to deliver the opening dialogue and I just remember being very nervous. Despite this I managed to perform the dialogue all the same.

Although the aforementioned two plays were really the pinnacle of my school play acting career, I did find myself appearing in the chorus of a Christmas gang show at a venue somewhere off the Kenton Road. This was thanks to me being an enthusiastic member of both the cubs (11th Kenton Mowgli) and the boy scouts.

At the time, I didn't realise that these early experiences of appearing in front of an audience must have been sowing some very early seeds in my brain. Seeds that would ultimately spur me on in later life to want to, by choice, present myself in front of a TV audience – sometimes on live TV programmes!

Paul B: I then asked Paul if there were any other influences in his childhood that might have inspired him to take an interest in wanting to appear on television:

Paul W: I can remember being taken to watch two pantomimes by my parents. In fact the first pantomime I recall seeing was in about 1963 or 1964. It was a production of *Aladdin* at the London Palladium which starred Cliff Richard (now, of course, Sir Cliff Richard), and the now much-missed comedian Arthur Askey. I really enjoyed the panto and thought it was very entertaining. I can vividly remember sitting in the stalls of the theatre next to my mum and her telling me that she had spotted one of the stars of the hit radio show *The Goon Show*, Michael Bentine, sitting a couple of rows in front of us. Well, during the interval a lot of people swarmed around him to get his autograph and mum sent me over as well. I must be honest and admit that I probably didn't really know who he was at the time, me being so young.

While my parents and I were standing outside the front of the Palladium before the show Cliff Richard came running past us and into the main foyer. He was wearing glasses, probably so as not to be recognised, but I remember my mum and I looking at each other and saying totally star-struck: 'That's Cliff Richard!'

The second pantomime my parents took me to see was at the Golders Green Hippodrome. It was *Cinderella*, and it starred the wonderful Dickie Henderson as Buttons. I can't remember who else was in the cast but I remember thinking it was marvellous.

Thinking back to Cliff Richard reminds me that my mum took me to the Odeon Cinema on Kingsbury High Road to see him starring in the film *Summer Holiday*, and I absolutely loved it! In those days you could stay in the cinema and watch the film twice – and that's what we did! We then did the same a year or so later when the Cliff Richard film *Wonderful Life* was released.

Paul B: I then pointed out to Paul that it is a happy coincidence that he now lives just a mile or so from

Elstree Studios where Cliff made the above-mentioned films in the early 1960s. Not only that, but being the same studios where Paul himself now regularly takes part in broadcasts of the Big Brother *spin-off show,* Big Brother's Big Mouth. *Okay, and one more coincidence, it is also the same studios where we both initially had our first meeting together regarding this book.*

So were Summer Holiday *and* Wonderful Life *the first experiences Paul had of being taken to the cinema?*

Paul W: No. There were two girls called Ann and Susan McCarthy who used to live next door to us in Farrer Road; and they took me on my first visit to the cinema when I was about nine years old. I was actually quite nervous – not of the girls, but of the experience of going to the cinema! The film was *Whistle Down the Wind*, which starred Hayley Mills and Alan Bates. I look back now and of course realise that it was a very good film.

Paul B: Listening to Paul speaking about family trips to both the theatre and the cinema then inspired me to ask whether he could recall any memorable family holidays:

Paul W: I can remember two family holidays in particular. I can't recall which came first, but I know that my parents once took myself and both my brothers, Simon and Martin, on a driving holiday to France and Belgium. We caught the ferry from Dover to Calais and it was a great holiday. I have this memory of us all in

Belgium sitting and eating waffles and ice cream with syrup. The other holiday that comes to mind is one etched on my memory for less happier reasons.

The day before we went away I was walking along the top of a wall in our front garden. It was a wall that had jagged edges positioned along the top. Well, I slipped off the wall, which was only about a foot high, and I cut myself really badly, blood was spurting out all down my left leg. This is yet another scar that I still have and it looks like a long ladder in a pair of tights!

Paul B: Having been shown the first scar he had been blessed with, I am delighted to report that I was spared a view of the second!

Paul W: It was never stitched, but instead, my parents just patched me up. Nowadays, of course, it would be stitched immediately. It was an awful long wound but my parents didn't want to cancel the holiday so they patched it up with Germolene and plasters and God knows what. Despite this I was in absolute agony and thinking to myself: What was I doing up on that wall? So the subsequent holiday, despite being in the South of France, wasn't very enjoyable because of the discomfort of the said accident.

Chapter Two
Football, Music and Preston's

My dad, Krulik Wilder, met my mum, Gloria Leigh, in 1951 at a club she used to attend with a lot of her female friends back in those days, it was called The Primrose Club. This was situated not too far from what is now Primrose Hill. My dad was also a regular at the club, and used to attend with the mates that he hung around with at the time. Then, following a courtship, they eventually married on Sunday 21st June 1953, which was my grandfather's birthday.

Because my dad was originally from Poland people think that his second name has been shortened. But it was, and still remains, Wilder. One imagines, however, that the 'W' was originally pronounced as a 'V'.

If you talk about heroes, then I would have to say that my No. 1 hero of all time was – and still is – my dad. He was a Holocaust survivor and he lost all of his family during the war. He was being held in a concentration camp when his dad died.

My dad was eventually liberated and brought over to the UK without knowing a soul and without being able to speak a single word of English. Just imagine at the tender age of 15 being taken to a strange country, being alone and how this must have felt. He went on to learn English and work first in Windermere in the Lake District and then in Cardross, about 30 miles from Glasgow.

Whilst living in the latter he learnt a trade, the trade in question being a watch repairer/watch maker. He then eventually came down to London and started a shop selling watches and built up a reasonable business which both my youngest brother, Martin, and I joined him in at a later stage. Indeed, it's only in recent years that the business has been disbanded. This parting was to result in my father retiring and my brother and myself going our separate ways.

My dad's story was later published in a book called *The Boys* by Martin Gilbert, and I don't think anything more can be admired than surviving what he went through.

I actually travelled with both my parents to dad's home town of Piotrkow in Poland, back in 1997. Dad showed me where he used to live and where both he and his dad used to work in a glass factory. Despite being some 65 years earlier, we were able to view a register which included both my dad and my grandfather's names in it.

Very upsetting, however, was the part of our visit where my dad showed us the area of his hometown where the German's used to kick him when he was just a little boy. I have nothing but admiration for him for what he had to endure.

Until very close to the date I was born, my mum, who married my dad at the tender of age of 18, worked for the Forestry Commission from the age of 15.

Paul B: Talking about his parents inspired Paul to produce a host of old photo albums which included photos of his much-missed grandparents:

Paul W: My grandparents, my mum's parents, Hymie and Lottie Leigh, were very special to me and I still miss them greatly. Because my dad's parents were killed in the Holocaust I obviously never met either of them and this is one of the many reasons why I became especially close to my other grandparents. They both hailed from the East End of London and later moved over to Wembley. I referred to them as grandma and grandpa, but my grandfather became affectionately called 'Gramps'.

I can remember being taken on several very enjoyable holidays by my grandparents, both with and without my two brothers, to Cliftonville, a seaside resort situated near to Margate in Kent. I recall that we always stayed at The Windsor Hall Hotel.

When my grandfather closed his jewellery shop in Hackney, he came to work with us in our wholesale jewellery business in Hatton Garden for a few years. So I was fortunate to work alongside him as well.

15

The night before my grandfather died I went to see him in hospital. He wasn't conscious and I don't think he was aware that I was even there. I just knew that I had to go there on my own to say goodbye. Although he died on Wednesday 17th November 1993, I still miss him a great deal. We had a great bond.

The year 1966 was to see me gain some early independence. I was 11 years old and myself and a group of friends started making daytrips up to London to visit all the various attractions, such as the Houses of Parliament, The Monument and Tower Bridge. In those days, despite the fact that we were such a young age, one felt safe and thought nothing of travelling around London as a group by bus and train without parental supervision. In fact we used to have a great time. I think I did more London sightseeing at that age than I do now!

My eleventh year also saw me discover a love for football and become a life-long supporter of my favourite football team, Arsenal. Like many boys, I chose my football team because it was also my dad's favourite team.

I can clearly recall making a red and white hat one day (Arsenal's colours) out of paper and glue (very *Blue Peter*-ish!) and then asking my dad when he was going to take me to watch a football match. He was surprised as he didn't even think I was interested in watching football – let alone accompanying him to watch an Arsenal game.

Paul B: What had really inspired Paul's interest in football was an event which arguably also inspired millions of other schoolboys to take an avid interest in the sport for the first time back in 1966 – The World Cup.

Paul W: My father and some of his mates managed to get tickets to watch the *The World Cup Final* which took place at the old Wembley Stadium. I remember that I was really, really upset not to have been able to accompany them. Instead, I watched the match on our then newly-purchased Colour TV set which was bought especially for *The World Cup Final*.

The first Arsenal football match that my dad took me to at their old Highbury Stadium was on Boxing Day 1966. I was so excited about the prospect of watching a real live football match; and the experience was further enhanced by the fact that Arsenal won against Southampton, 4–1! Two goals each were scored by John Radford and the late, great winger 'wee Geordie' George Armstrong, who was one of my favourite Arsenal players of all time.

The following year, following a huge amount of begging to my father, we purchased season tickets to watch Arsenal. We would then go on to buy season tickets for the next twenty years and would go to many of the cup finals that Arsenal took part in.

We used to have seats in the lower tier of the East Stand at Arsenal's ground and this gave us a great view. By now a convert of the Arsenal faith, I had started to keep a scrapbook about the club which I still have to this day stored in the loft somewhere.

In my childhood visits to watch Arsenal play, one of the fondest memories I have is of the strange, mixed aroma of foods that used to waft around the ground. There was the smelly hot dogs that you could buy (without onions, as I have always hated them!) and the strange stench of Bovril! The smells of food were just another aspect which used to help contribute to the enjoyable atmosphere that there was at the games I attended with my dad and later my grandfather.

Being a small 11–year–old, however, made entering and leaving the Highbury ground very scary and I must admit that I disliked all the pushing and shoving that went on from the crowd. Despite this I didn't see too much trouble from any of the home or away fans at the ground.

As I got older I started to take Gramps to Arsenal matches. I used to pick him up in my car, take us to the ground stopping off along the way for fish and chips at the Arsenal Fish Bar, a restaurant on Blackstock Road in Highbury. Gramps always put loads of salt on his fish and chips and I can remember that on one occasion he accidentally picked up the sugar instead of the salt! He covered his fish in sugar. I said that I would ask them to change it but he insisted on scraping off the sugar and eating all of the fish and chips!

I enjoyed taking Gramps to matches and I loved to see the joy in his face when we went on those outings. We had a great bond together and I always felt it was the perfect way for me to help pay him back for all the help and kindness he had shown to me as I was growing up. Watching Arsenal play became a massive passion for me. I still watch them play on Sky, but these days I only ever occasionally attend games.

Paul B: With the opportunity to appear in the audience of Top of the Pops *having seemingly played such an important role in Paul's life at the age of 17, I then asked Paul just how much of an important part music played during his childhood:*

Paul W: I was and still am a massive fan of The Beatles and their albums continue to get played on my iPod more than anything else! If I am relaxing or sunbathing I will invariably click onto the albums *Revolver* or *Rubber Sole*.

I used to visit a fantastic department store called Gamages, which is sadly no-longer with us. If you mention Gamages to anyone who remembers London, specifically Holborn, in the 1960s and 1970s they'll say: 'Oh I used to love that store!' There was only the one store but it was, in my opinion, the greatest ever department store.

I can remember going to Gamages on my own several times in the school holidays and they had the most fantastic record department. You could go to the counter in the department and say: 'I'd like to listen to such and such record,' and you'd then go into one of their little sound booths, put a set of headphones on and the record would be played for you and you could then decide if you wanted to buy it or not.

The first 7 inch single record I ever bought was from Gamages back in 1964 when I was only 9 years old. It was *5-4-3-2-1* by Manfred Mann. I paid for it with the pocket money I had accumulated. The record was 6/8d (six shillings and 8 pennies old money), which is just over 30p in today's money. My first album or LP (as they used to call them) I had was a requested gift for Christmas 1964 which was called *Beatles For Sale* – and I played and played this record to death!

If I think back now I realise that it must have been seeing the likes of The Beatles, Cliff Richard and The Rolling Stones appearing on television on shows like *Ready Steady Go!* And *Thank Your Lucky Stars* that made me want to become a pop star. Unfortunately, I discovered quite early on that I can't sing a note! And I can remember when I was about 16 or 17 thinking: 'Okay, well I can't sing but maybe I can become a song writer'. It was just anything to be in the music business.

I also think that one of the other reasons I was so keen on becoming a pop singer was having watched all the black and white footage on TV of girls screaming at groups like The Beatles at London Airport and I thought 'I want the same kind of female adoration!'.

Recalling Radio 1 starting in 1967 and the first DJ heard on the station, Tony Blackburn, playing the first record:

Flowers In The Rain by The Move. This was quite an event for me, being such a big music fan.

The only regret or minor gripe I have about my childhood is that I was the eldest of three brothers. Some of my friends that had elder brothers and sisters used to take them to see groups like The Beatles live; but because I was young and there was no-way my parents would let me go alone to see a Beatles concert, I never did get to see them.

In either 1972/73 I took my brothers to see the likes of Slade etc. – because I was the elder brother. My younger brother still has fond memories of me carrying him on my shoulders after seeing Slade in concert at the Empire Pool in Wembley.

Paul B: Having discovered about Paul's compulsion to buy the latest records as a child, I then asked how he managed to supplement his pocket money in order to afford all the latest hits:

Paul W: Well, when I was about 12 years old my Uncle Peter said: 'How about you come and stack shelves for me in my shop after school to earn some extra money?' I agreed, and so I used to come home from school, get the train from Preston Road to Wembley Park, which was one stop, and then walk to the shop from Wembley Park Station.

My uncle's shop was called Preston's Food Fare and it was an old fashioned grocery store that was situated on a row of shops which was opposite the Associated Rediffusion television studios.

Paul B: Post the Associated Rediffusion years, the studios became the temporary home of the one-time London weekend ITV franchise-holder, LWT (London Weekend Television), who made programmes there including: On the Buses *and* Please, Sir! *And while the names Associated Rediffusion and LWT might not mean much to the younger generation, their old studios in Wembley Park, will, for they have since become Fountain Studios and are now, at the time of writing, the home of some of the biggest TV hits in the UK. These include:* The X-Factor *and* Britain's Got Talent. *So already the lure of television was casting its beckoning shadow over Paul's world.*

Paul W: I can remember my Uncle Peter getting me Alan 'Fluff' Freeman's autograph when he came into the shop one day. Indeed, my Uncle used to tell me that several well-known stars used to pop into the shop because it was situated so close to the studios.

Little did I know, at that point in my life as I worked in my uncle's shop opposite the old Associated Rediffusion studios, that I would one day enter the studio complex and appear in a game show for Channel 5, and come so close to winning a life-changing amount of money!

Paul B: A barmitzvah is a very, very important event in a Jewish boy's life which takes place when he is 13 years old in a synagogue on Shabbat (the Jewish

Sabbath – Saturday) morning. This coincides with his Jewish birthday. This is usually within a week or so of his English birthday.

Paul W: My barmitzvah took place on Saturday 16th March 1968 at Kenton Synagogue, where I would later marry my better half, Suzanne.

At your barmitzvah one has to stand centre stage, so to speak, on the bimah (prayer altar) and recite Maftir and Haftorah (a segment of the Torah, the Jewish book of law and a section of the Prophets) in Hebrew. You have months and months of tuition to help you learn this segment. This comes more natural to some boys – but it didn't to me! I well remember receiving considerable coaching and learning it parrot fashion.

However, as a 13-year-old I was quite small (in fact I had to stand on a box in order to be seen) and very, very nervous! My voice had not broken as yet, so all in all it was a bit of an ordeal for me. However, everybody congratulated me afterwards and a big party, as is tradition, was held the following day. It was a very joyous occasion which, for me, was only slightly marred by the fact that I had to make a speech! The speech was written and read by myself because certain people had to be thanked.

The first dog that my mum bought for the family was in 1968 not long after my barmitzvah. Sandy was a Golden Labrador and a puppy at the time she first came to live with us. She was a gorgeous dog and when she died we soon adopted an absolute lunatic of a dog, a Red Setter, which we called Lucy. I can say that my life-long love of dogs began back then.

A few years after our daughter Melody was born, we were unfortunately told that we could not have any more children so decided we should get a dog. We drove to Herne Bay in Kent to visit a dog breeder and saw the cutest West Highland Terrier puppies that were barely two weeks old. The breeder picked out one of them for us and said she would be suited for our little family. How right she was, we collected her about six weeks later and named her 'Chloe'. Her temperament was perfect and we had 14 very happy years with her until she became so ill that we had to have her put down. It broke our hearts and we were all in tears that day.

Because both of my wife, Suzanne, and my various extra work engagements, which can be offered at short notice, it has not been practical for us to have another dog.

Chapter Three
Fan-Dabi-Double-Dozi

Taking my GCE O'Levels at the age of 16 I then entered the Sixth Form in 1971 and, to be honest, didn't really have a clue what I wanted to do, having no direction at all. I had been helping in my dad's business during the school holidays. It was a wholesale jewellery firm and, although it wasn't exciting, I did enjoy the money.

Only taking a handful of subjects in the Sixth Form, by the November I was getting a bit bored with it so my dad said: 'Why don't you come and work in the business? That way you can earn some money.' Well, by then I was really starting to enjoy my social life and because I had been very shy I was a bit of a late starter when it came to having girlfriends. Now I wanted to make up for lost time! Going out, of course, costs money so I decided that I'd had enough of school, left and went straight into the family business.

Not long after I had started working in my dad's business in November 1971 I found myself sitting in the back of his showroom being given the hugely-uninspiring job of wrapping parcels with brown paper. In those days I was the equivalent of a post- room boy.

To relieve the boredom of this unrewarding task I used to sit there when my dad wasn't looking and write song lyrics down on the brown paper. My mate Melvyn used to play the guitar and he put some tunes to my lyrics, however, it was never anything that was going to set the world alight! At the back of my mind there was always this hope that maybe, just maybe, I could make it as a song writer because Melvyn and I thought the songs were fantastic. In fact we did offer up some of our best efforts to song publishers. I used to ring up the publishers and deliver them a very business-like patter and really lay on the charm but, unfortunately, this never got us anywhere.

Paul B: So, I asked Paul, who were the song writers of the day who became his inspiration:

Paul W: The greatest songwriters were of course John Lennon and Paul McCartney; but I also loved the songs of Ray Davies, the lead singer with The Kinks. Davies wrote some brilliantly quintessentially English lyrics about Sunny Afternoon's and Waterloo Sunset's, an absolute genius. I am also a really big fan of Elton John and Bernie Taupin, great songwriters.

Paul B: Sensing that Paul has never really got over the disappointment of not becoming the Gary Barlow of his day, I quickly decided to change the subject to other passions that took his fancy back in his teenage years:

Paul W: I was very, very happy at home but my biggest wish was to pass my driving test. Everyone said that if you wanted to pass your driving test quickly then you've had to have experience of the road. A one hour lesson a week just wasn't enough. So my grandfather, who had the patience of a saint, agreed to sit with me in rush hour traffic from Wembley to Hatton Garden twice a day for 3–4 months while I gained the extra driving practice. The extra practice obviously paid off, because I passed my driving test after just 12 official lessons. I was just so focused it was all I wanted to do.

I was 17 in the March and I passed my test in the July of that year. I can vividly remember being in my room before taking my test and playing a record (*Suffragette City* by David Bowie from the *Ziggy Stardust* album) 17 times in a row – don't ask me why! To me learning to drive was one of the best things I had achieved in my life to that point.

My grandfather then decided to buy a new car and I was very lucky because he passed on to me the Ford Escort 1100 that he had given me all that extra valuable driving experience in. So that was my first car and I remember customising it by putting on it stickers of the likes of Mickey Mouse and Dougal from *The Magic Roundabout!* How sad that I was thinking that I was the bees knees in my love machine with pictures of Dougal all over the car!

The next mad obsession I had was to own my own flat. I think I was about 22 when I first heard about a flat in Wembley Park. It was a little one-bedroom flat at the side of the Town Hall on King's Drive. It cost £16,000, which was a lot of money in those days. Regrettably, the estate agent kept me hanging about for a year and the sale fell through. I was bitterly disappointed. The flat was apparently owned by a couple who, I believe, were originally planning to get divorced. They must have had a change of heart about splitting up because they also changed their minds about selling the flat. While I may have been happy for the couple's decision to get back together, I was, of course, devastated about losing the chance to own a flat of my own.

Fate was kinder to me a year or so later, however, when a studio flat came on the market in Stanmore, which was a much more salubrious area. I went to view it and immediately fell in love with it – or as much as you can fall in love with a flat! I think I agreed to purchase it for the grand total of £18,000.

Then, about ten or so months later a two-bedroom flat came on the market in Stanmore and I thought: 'I want to go for this,' so I put my studio flat on the market and sold it for £22,750! I had made a £4,750 profit in ten months and thought: 'my goodness, this beats working!' I bought the two-bedroom flat in Stanmore Hill for £30,000 and took out a £15,000 mortgage on the property. It was incredibly spacious and that really became my bachelor pad and where I made up for lost time with members of the opposite sex – by then my shyness had really gone!

Not far from my new two-bedroom bachelor pad there was the most fantastic nightclub called the Middlesex and Herts. Country Club and it was situated on the Harrow Weald/Stanmore border. I think the same company who owned the nightclub also had a sister nightclub in Essex called the Epping Forest Country Club. I became a member and, as I only lived around the corner, I spent most of my time there, when I wasn't working, propping up the piano in the piano bar and getting very drunk. I didn't like the loud disco music in there which is why I was always frequenting the piano bar. Some great girls were met there and some good times were had!

One morning in 1977 while I was at work the phone rang and the voice on the other end of the line asked to speak to Willie Wilder (Willie Wilder was a nickname I had at the time – but that's another story!). Well, not surprisingly, I at first thought it was someone playing a prank on me. I was told the caller was from Radio 1 and they asked me to go on air on Simon Bates' quiz show, *Meet Your Match*. I then remembered that I had applied under the name of Willie Wilder to be a contestant on a quiz show on Tony Blackburn's radio show. Now Simon Bates' show, complete with quiz, was in its slot. I had completely forgotten that I had applied!

I then asked the caller when I was due to take part in the quiz and I received the reply: 'Tomorrow'. My heart nearly missed a thousand beats – already I was feeling nervous! As it turned out I didn't have cause to be nervous as the experience was great fun and I won the quiz for three days running! Sadly, I lost on the Friday. But, for my efforts, I won a t-shirt and a selection of the latest music albums.

Appearing on Simon Bates' radio show did not signify the first time I had taken part in a radio quiz. Previously, I had twice been on a radio quiz on London radio station, Capital Radio, on former Radio Caroline DJ Dave Cash's daily quiz show. Cash's quiz was wittily entitled 'Cash on Delivery'. Despite not winning, I enjoyed the experience because contestants actually got the chance to take part in the studio at Capital Radio instead of just via the phone. My radio quiz show success was reported in a newspaper called the Harrow Observer, and the article featured the headline:

'Come tomorrow' said the BBC

The article also featured a small photo of me with long hair and big glasses.

Having just looked back at the article in a scrapbook that I recently found in the loft of our current Elstree home, it is interesting to read that my attempts to become a song lyricist are also featured. They also included my appeal to find someone who could help me set my lyrics to music. The paper, in a usual local paper-type-way added:

'Is there an Elton John to team up with Harrow's potential Bernie Taupin?'

Around March 1983, I decided to take a holiday on my own to Eilat, Israel, as I didn't have a girlfriend at the time. I stayed in a hotel called the Sonesta. I think this hotel is now on Egyptian soil and has since been renamed.

Two girls, Naomi and Marsha, who I knew, were, by strange coincidence, also on holiday there and staying in the same hotel. Anyway, word soon got round that the Hollywood actress and model Brooke Shields was staying in the Sonesta. Brooke was in Israel to shoot scenes for a new film entitled Sahara. I am pretty sure she was only 18 years old at the time but despite this she was a very big star.

One day Brooke was playing tennis and I think everyone staying in the hotel (possibly the whole resort were watching her play). I said to Naomi: 'Before the end of the holiday I am going to have my photo taken with Brooke Shields.' Not surprisingly she laughed, with good reason, as it was going to be a neigh-on impossible quest given that the actress in question was seemingly always surrounded by a team of burly built bodyguards – oh, and her mum! And it was more than obvious to me that it was going to be even harder to get past her mum than the bodyguards! Anyway, I managed it. One day both Naomi and I were near to an area in the hotel where Brooke had hired a suite, when suddenly she walked out wearing a very skimpy vest and shorts. I was dumbstruck but said: 'Excuse me Brooke' (even now I blush at my cheek for using her first name!), 'would you mind if I had my photo taken with you?' And, to my delight and total amazement, she said: 'Oh sure.' I've still got the photo taken by Naomi and it's become the pride of my collection.

Paul B: At this point Paul showed me the prized photo in question. I couldn't help but notice what a great couple they looked. No, seriously, the two of them together looked as though they could feasibly have been a couple, if you didn't know otherwise. I mentioned my observation to Paul. He smiled and without a pause agreed!

Paul W: I can remember making my way back to my hotel room with a huge smile on my face. Taking a bath a short while later I lay back in the water, rubbed my eyes and stared up at a crack in the ceiling. I started fantasising to myself (no, not that kind of fantasising – well maybe!). Thoughts entered my head such as, 'wouldn't it be brilliant if Brooke wanted to take me back to Hollywood with her.' But it wasn't to be. I was, as it turned out, fated to end up in Borehamwood – not Hollywood!

In was during the same holiday that I met two more stars. The stars in question were the husband and wife comedy double act, The Krankies. The duo (Ian and Janette Tough) were staying at the same hotel as the girls and myself (oh, and not forgetting Brooke, of course!). I met them both in the hotel bar and I got talking to them. We got on very well together and before long we were all drinking together into the wee small hours and soon became good friends.

When we all got back to the UK, Ian and Janette invited me to watch them recording their TV series, *The Krankies Klub*, for LWT (London Weekend Television). So every Friday evening I went along to LWT's studios on the South Bank in London to watch the shows being recorded.

Before each recording I used to join Ian and Janette in the studio bar for a drink (and after the recordings as well!). Whilst drinking with them in the bar I got the opportunity to meet many of the guests who appeared with them in the series. These included comedian Jimmy Cricket, who was a very nice guy, and the much-missed comedian, impersonator and one-time comedy partner of Les Dennis, Dustin Gee.

I used to sit in the studio audience for the recordings and some weeks I took my brother, Martin, and on a couple of occasions I even took my girlfriend of the time. In fact I can clearly recall the then Radio 1 DJ Tony Blackburn, who was a guest on an edition of the show, trying to chat my girlfriend up in the bar!

Prior to the recordings Ian and Janette used to do the audience warm-ups for the show together. Each week, without fail, Janette used to point me out to the other members of the audience and say: 'That's our friend Paul Wilder. He kissed Brooke Shields you know!' It was really funny and I, of course, was in my element!

I can also remember going to a famous London restaurant, and a favourite haunt of well-known actors and actresses, with Ian and Janette called The Ivy. I couldn't believe it, there was little old me eating with two of this country's most popular light entertainment performers in what was the late Noel Coward's favourite restaurant!

The same year, 1983, I took my then girlfriend for a long weekend in Great Yarmouth in Norfolk. This was the resort where The Krankies were appearing in summer season that year. We went backstage to meet them at the theatre they were appearing at. I can remember that the comedian Duncan 'Chase me' Norvelle was also appearing on the same bill as Ian and Janette.

During the weekend Ian, Janette, my girlfriend and I all went out to eat at a restaurant one night. We then moved to one of the bars in the resort where all the various performers appearing in the town would congregate after their respective shows. The madcap comedian Freddie Starr turned up at the bar whilst we were there.

During the period when I was regularly seeing Ian and Janette I decided to try and write some lyrics for a forthcoming album that they were releasing called *Krankies Go To Hollywood* (my song-writing ambitions have never left me!). The track I wrote lyrics for was called *Krankies Rap*. I am not sure, but I believe some of my lyrics were actually used in the finished song! What a claim to fame, eh!

I stayed in touch with Ian and Janette for a couple of years and we had a great time. In fact they even attended my brother Martin's wedding to Mandy as guests and they went down a storm! They came to both the ceremony at the synagogue and the wedding reception. In fact we still have a video of The Krankies joining in a rousing version of *New York, New York* which was played by the band at the wedding led by Ray McVay.

Incidentally, I had the honour of being best man at Martin's wedding. This was at the height of my days of being single. I recall taking as my guest to the wedding a 'busty' waitress from a nightclub that I was frequenting at the time. A few of dad's friends' eyes popped out on being introduced to the afore-mentioned waitress! As best man I was, of course, required to deliver a speech. When the toastmaster called me up onto the stage, I was nowhere to be found. I had already written and prepared my speech but I was well and truly as inebriated as a newt! I did, however, eventually deliver the speech in true comedic drunkenness and, I am proud to say, had the room in hysterics!

When I started to see Suzanne I took her one weekend to see The Krankies in summer season in the resort of Bournemouth in 1985 – I know how to impress a girl! In 2004 I was very upset to hear that Janette had suffered a bad accident after falling ten feet off a pantomime beanstalk in Glasgow. The Krankies were starring in a production of *Jack and the Beanstalk* at the city's Pavilion Theatre and Janette fell off the large prop during a matinee show.

I contacted Ian and Janette again and I was delighted when they called me at home one day – we had a good chat and reminisced about old times.

Paul B: The topic of conversation then changed direction as Paul then began to recall the first time that he met his then future wife Suzanne:

Paul W: I first met my future wife, Suzanne Keyes, at a very smart/bar restaurant in St John's Wood called Rosetti. Once a week, Rosetti's used to get mobbed with youngsters from the local area. They had a smart restaurant upstairs and it was a great place to meet people. I remember taking Suzanne out for a drink and that I said something to her like: 'You're a lovely girl and the kind of girl I'd like to marry'.

A couple of years later Suzanne and I met again at the Middlesex and Herts. Country Club, and I think I was about the age of 28 when we first started going out properly. I don't know why Suzanne stuck with me as she will tell you that she remembers that at the time I used to be all over the place! I used to wear this dreadful bright yellow jacket and my friends used to send me up and call me John Travolta because of the clothes that I wore during that period!

Paul B: After hearing Paul's recollections of meeting Suzanne I was, of course, very keen to find out what her initial thoughts were of Paul!:

Suzanne: When I first met Paul he was dressed as if he thought he was a cross between John Travolta in Saturday Night Fever *and Don Johnson in* Miami Vice. *Unfortunately he was neither of these people – but he made me laugh because he thought he was!*

Paul W: I remember the first time Suzanne took me home to meet her parents Jeannette and Melvyn. They were sitting watching the American TV soap *Dallas* as we arrived. *Dallas*, as you will probably know, was one of the biggest shows on TV back then. Meeting a girlfriend's parents was always a daunting experience for me, but I can honestly say that meeting Suzanne's parents was a joy.

I was particularly fond of my mother-in-law Jeannette who was a very glamorous lady. She suffered the crippling disease of multiple sclerosis with amazing dignity and never complained despite being confined to a wheelchair for the last few years of her life. Sadly, Jeannette passed away suddenly in her sleep from a heart attack on the 1st October 2008. I could not have asked for a better mother-in-law and she is more than sadly missed.

Finally, at the age of 30, Suzanne and I were married at Kenton Synagogue on Sunday 5th January 1986. We had a lovely reception at the Rainbow Rooms in Kensington and it was a really wonderful day.

Paul B: Being aware of Paul's great sense of humour, I asked him whether he had been tempted into adding a few jokes into his wedding speech:

Paul W: I was – and did! During my speech I turned to Suzanne and said: 'Will you still love me when I look like this?' At which point I put on an ugly old man's mask which had grey straggly hair hanging down at the side. Suzanne still recalls this with eye-rolling embarrassment to this day!

Paul B: So, jokes aside, I wondered how Suzanne views Paul after all these years:

Suzanne: Paul is a very kind person. He is a very loving and caring husband, a wonderful father and a good son and an exceptionally kind son-in-law. He is a loyal and good friend who I love very much.

Paul W: Suzanne and I honeymooned in St Lucia at a resort called Couples, which was an all-inclusive hotel. The moment we arrived I went straight to the bar and ordered a large Scotch and Coke. Not only did I not have to pay, but the barman also offered me a Johnnie Walker Black Label (a premier whiskey).

Couples was one of the first all-inclusive Caribbean resorts back in 1986 and being partial to whiskey back then the traditional first night of our honeymoon did not exactly turn out as planned! The saying 'A whiskey makes you frisky' did not apply that night – in my case it was a case of whiskey makes you sleepy! Our honeymoon, incidentally, was the very first and last time that I ever did any water skiing. I wasn't very successful at it but I at least had a go! Our honeymoon also went down in history as being the one and only time that Suzanne and I rode a horse. It sounds very romantic us both riding horses together along a sun-drenched beach with the sea gently lapping on the sand – but in actual fact we were both (Suzanne, in particular) really petrified!

Suzanne and I moved to the first of our, to date, three houses in Elstree during the summer of 1986. I can remember that during our first weekend living there that we didn't have a washing machine plumbed in. As a result we decided to call into a launderette in nearby Borehamwood close to BBC Elstree where *EastEnders* is taped.

As we were going into the launderette we bumped into the actor Leslie Grantham (aka Dirty Den from *EastEnders*) coming out armed with a big bag of washing. I was amazed! EastEnders had only started the previous year and the soap, as well as Leslie and his character, were really big news at the time. I remember saying to Suzanne what an excellent introduction we had been given to moving into an area which continues to be known as Britain's Hollywood because of its film and television heritage.

Our daughter Melody was born on a very hot afternoon on Friday 10th July 1987 at Watford General Hospital. As previously-mentioned, unfortunately, after she was born we discovered that we couldn't have any more children so Melody is, of course, extra special to us and we are very, very proud of her.

Melody only likes to be called Mel and all her friends know her as Mel. However, I still call her Melody. Just after she was born I used to drive everyone mad with the joke that Suzanne and I (as her parents) were the Melody-makers! Melody will hate me for mentioning that!

When Melody reached the age of 12 we had a special batmitzvah for her and celebrated at a lovely country hotel, called the Grimsdyke Hotel, which is situated on the Harrow Weald/Stanmore border. (A girl can have a batmitzvah – sort of an equivalent of a boy's barmitzvah). We made this a night to remember and even booked a Bee Gees tribute band that really got everybody up on their feet dancing!

Me aged just 18 months.

With mum in our Ford Anglia in 1956.

Mum, Dad and I on holiday
in Bournemouth in 1956.

Yee Ha! On holiday with 'Gramps'
in Cliftonville, Kent, around 1957.

With my younger brothers, Simon and Martin, in 1963.

Rock On! A would-be rock star in October 1973.

With the lovely 18-year-old Brooke Shields in March 1983.

It was 'Fan-dabi-double-dozi' when I met The Krankies in 1983.

Jimmy Krankie (Janette Tough) plays the ventriloquist's dummy as we mess around in Eilat, 1983.

Drinking Buddies! Ian Krankie (Ian Tough) and yours truly in Great Yarmouth in July 1983.

What a Carry On! Me with bubbly Babs Windsor in 1988.

Queen lead guitarist Brian May played at one of my favourite gigs in 1973. This photo was taken around 1988.

I have bumped into Des O'Connor a couple of times since this photo was taken around 1988.

Pictured here in the *Every Second Counts'* Green Room after the recording with host Paul Daniels and the lovely Debbie McGee.

You know it makes sense, Rodders! With David Jason and Nicholas Lyndhurst at a Water Rats Ball in 1990.

I wasn't *All Clued Up* like Suzanne when we won £450 with 'Diddy' David Hamilton on his Sunday afternoon quiz show.

Strictly fun! I was thrilled to meet Bruce Forsyth at the *Takeover Bid* rehearsals despite not making it onto an actual edition of the show.

What a clever disguise the beard was! With my friend David Phillips and the late Lennie Bennett at Anglia Television's Norwich studios for *Lucky Ladders*.

Here's me as 'Gary Keyes' on the set of Les Dawson's *Fast Friends*.

With the American author Kitty Kelley. We got on famously in the Green Room – she thought I was a 'real' celebrity.

With mum and dad on our emotional visit to Piotrokow (my dad's home town) in Poland, September 1997.

One of the all-time
great football legends,
Sir Bobby Charlton.

They think it's all over
… it is now!
The phrase that has been
repeated millions of times
since *The World Cup 1966*
hero Sir Geoff Hurst
completed his hat trick.

Football legend and
Match of the Day host
Gary Lineker.

Dad Krulik finally 'doing
lunch' with American
comedian Jackie Mason at
the appropriately named
Fortnum & Mason!

Meeting Oasis frontman Liam Gallagher
at a private party turned me into a gibbering wreck!

I was partnered with
The Bill's Joy Brook
on the show and met
the late *EastEnders'*
Ross Davidson on
It's Anybody's Guess.

Together with my friends Henry Felstein and Northern Soul star
Lorraine Silver we possessed a wealth of celebrity knowledge,
but we still lost on the Lisa Rogers-hosted game show *Celebrity Addicts*.

With the much-missed
comedian and game show host
Bob Monkhouse in 2000.

Actress Pauline Quirke and I share
a love of the canteen at *The Bill*.

With future *Strictly Come Dancing*
contestant Rachel Stevens at BBC
Television Centre in 2001.

Gettng on very well with one-time
Jet Set host Eamonn Holmes just
before the BBC banned me from
appearing on the show!

Chapter Four
Every Second Counts

I always had it fixed in my mind that I wanted to be on television but I realised that I didn't have any specific talent. I couldn't sing (I was and still am tone deaf!), I couldn't play an instrument and I couldn't write any songs successfully and, as far as I knew, I couldn't act! So what could I do to be on television? I just didn't know. But a couple of years after I got married, and while our daughter, Melody, was still very young, Suzanne and I happened to be watching a quiz show one Friday night called *Every Second Counts*.

Paul B: Every Second Counts *was a perfect example of the type of cheap and cheerful light entertainment game show that the BBC used to make and broadcast in the 1980s. The show came from the same BBC department that produced such shows as* Blankety Blank *and* Bob's Full House. *This was in a decade which, one could quite confidently argue, was the last decade of British TV's golden age.*

Every Second Counts, *like the previous latter two-named quiz shows were low on budget but high on entertainment value and personality. They were all hosted by talented exponents of the art of quiz and game shows and who were masters of working with the public.* Blankety Blank *was hosted firstly by radio DJ and then future TV chat show host Terry Wogan, and then by the much-missed Les Dawson.* Bob's Full House, *meanwhile, was hosted by one of the King's of the genre: Bob Monkhouse.*

In the case of Every Second Counts, *our genial host was none other than the TV magician Paul Daniels who had become Mr Saturday Night and was originally propelled to TV stardom thanks to* The Paul Daniels Magic Show. *It's fair to say that Daniels' magic show will be a British TV magic show that will never be beaten or bettered. It gave a chance for the TV magician, who hailed from the north, to not only display his talent for slight of hand but also his natural ability to prove that he had a great comic timing and a wonderful rapport with the British public. One can only surmise that this is what must have inspired BBC TV executives to give the master of magic the chance to host* Every Second Counts.

What isn't widely-known about Every Second Counts *is that originally two pilots were taped and never broadcast before the series was handed to Daniels. The first host to try his hand at the show was former* Generation Game *presenter Larry Grayson, whilst the second was TV astrologer Russell Grant.*

How interesting it would be to have seen the tapes of Grayson and Grant's versions of the show!

With Paul Daniels as host, Every Second Counts *was to run for 142 editions from February 1986 until October 1993. Daniels would then helm* Wipeout *before later handing the reins to Bob Monkhouse. With such success, it seems a real mystery as to why the BBC or another broadcaster hasn't created a revamped version of* Every Second Counts *in more recent years.*

The format of Every Second Counts *was simple: three couples, mainly newly-weds (lots of comic potential for Daniels to explore with honeymoon disasters etc.), acted as contestants on the show. There were two desks for each couple, one at the front (known as the driving seat) and the other situated directly behind. Contestants from each couple took it in turns to answer questions seated at the front desk (the driving seat) whilst the other contestant would sit at the desk behind and secretly plan the break-up of their marriage as their partner gradually failed to successfully answer a host of questions posed by Paul. Although, of course, I am being unfair! Just occasionally contestants would answer questions correctly. But when contestants didn't answer their answers correctly their versions were invariably funny and gave something for Daniels to crack a joke about!*

After the first half of the show, contestants would change places. The winners were, obviously, the couple who had accumulated the most time during the show would then have the chance to win a holiday. But it didn't matter if they didn't. If couples had been there as contestants, then an Every Second Counts *clock was theirs for the taking! It was all light-hearted fun, no-one got hurt and millions were entertained.*

Meanwhile, back to the plot …

Paul W: At the end of one edition of *Every Second Counts* the continuity announcer read out a request for couples who were interested in appearing on the next series of the show. An address was displayed on the screen for couples to write to (enclosing an SAE, of course!) for an application form. I turned to Suzanne and said: 'Shall we apply to go on that as contestants?' After a little persuading she agreed and we wrote off for an application form. An application form duly arrived and I filled it in – the first of many that I have since completed!

Every quiz or game show application form asks you to write down any funny stories that you have about your honeymoon night etc. The funny story that I added to the application form was about our wedding day:

During a Jewish wedding held in a synagogue the man takes a sip from a cup of wine before offering it to his bride to do the same. Well, before the wedding Suzanne said to me: 'Whatever you do, don't spill any wine on my wedding dress,' well, of course, me being me, I did and that wasn't the ideal start to our marriage!

The researchers liked the story. In fact a good tip for anyone wanting to go on these types of shows is that the producers and researchers like funny stories that will instantly catch their attention on the application form and that the host or presenter of the show can then make fun of during the recording! Another thing I soon realised was that for shows like *Every Second Counts* they weren't looking for the most academic of people, just people who had a good personality, sense of humour and would ultimately be entertaining on the programme.

But it was many months before we were asked to go for an audition at BBC Television Centre. The audition, which took place on Friday 25th November 1988, seemed to go very well but they dampened our enthusiasm a little by reminding us that they were seeing many other couples as well.

One morning I came downstairs and found a letter on the mat with a BBC logo on the envelope. I opened it, read it and couldn't believe what it said. I rushed to Suzanne and regaled her with the contents of the BBC's letter: 'I can't believe it, they actually want us to be contestants on *Every Second Counts*!' After receiving our letter of acceptance from the *Every Second Counts'* production team, all I could think about was: I'm going to be on primetime BBC television!

Interestingly, by the time we received a letter telling us we had actually been accepted to appear on an edition of the show, it had been practically a whole year from when the initial request for would-be contestants to come forward.

The date of the recording of *Every Second Counts* that we actually appeared on (we had previously been to BBC Television Centre on Wednesday 18th January 1989 to be a standby couple) was Monday 23rd January 1989. Although the eventual programme wasn't broadcast until Friday 2nd June of that year – which was a long while to wait when you were desperate to see yourself on television!

On the recording day Suzanne and I made our way to the BBC Television Centre in West London. The production team wanted the three couples who were taking part as contestants there early for a meet-and-greet and a full rehearsal. When we arrived we were taken to the hospitality area and introduced to the other two couples taking part in the show. Paul Daniels himself came in and introduced himself and was very friendly. We then all had lunch together prior to a full rehearsal in the studio.

I can recall that Paul Daniels asked one of the girls during a break in the rehearsal what the time was, so naturally she went to look at her watch – which was gone! Paul had managed, without any of us realising, to take the watch off her when he initially met her. We all fell about laughing and this really helped to relax us. This, and all the other little tricks he was doing throughout the afternoon really put us at ease.

After the rehearsal we were taken to make-up during which time the audience began to file into the studio and took their places in the seating area. I must admit that by this stage I was feeling quite nervous. Here we were in the world famous BBC Television Centre about to appear on one of BBC1's biggest game shows of its day – so is it any wonder!

I remember deliberately wearing a bright jacket and odd socks hoping that this would get a mention from Paul Daniels – which it did! So even back then I had it all pre-planned. I am always especially conscious about what I am going to wear on a television show, especially on discussion shows like *Big Brother's Big Mouth*.

With Suzanne and I and our fellow contestants in our places, the studio audience safely seated and Paul Daniels and the team ready to start the show I knew it was too late to back out. I was going to have to make my nerves work for me, not against me!

Paul B: I then asked Suzanne what memories she had of taking part in Every Second Counts:

Suzanne: My abiding memory is that I answered all of my questions right and that Paul answered all of his questions wrong! Paul was too busy looking into the camera and not concentrating on his questions, whereas my competitive spirit came out and I was answering my questions correctly.

Paul W: I think we were the second couple knocked out. I understand that the couple who won the show went on to win the star prize which I believe was a holiday.

After the show, Suzanne and I, and the other two couples, all had a drink with Paul Daniels and his wife – the lovely Debbie McGee. We had a few friends in the studio audience and they were allowed by the BBC to come with us to the Green Room for a drink. Finally, Suzanne and I had photos taken with Paul and Debbie. It was just such an amazing day.

The moment that Suzanne and I got home I said to her: 'I want to go on more shows like that,' Suzanne replied: 'Do what you want' – which is what she still says now! She has always been very supportive of me. My desire and quest for TV fame was now fully born! When the show was finally broadcast it was watched by 11 million viewers.

The next game show I applied to take part in was *Strike It Lucky*, which, at the time, was made by Thames Television for ITV and hosted by Michael Barrymore. I applied for Suzanne and myself to take part in the show on Tuesday 31st January 1989. We were subsequently given an audition at Thames TV's studios on Euston Road in London, on Tuesday 10th July 1990. Sadly, we were not accepted onto the show. Incidentally, we failed a second time to make it onto the show when we later auditioned at Thames' then studios in Teddington, Middlesex, on Thursday 14th March 1991.

The next show I actually appeared on was called *Chain Letters*. I auditioned for this on Tuesday 2nd May 1989 at Tyne Tees' London office. I later discovered on Tuesday 13th June, while Suzanne, Melody and I were on holiday in Cyprus, that I had been accepted to be a contestant on the show. I recall that prior to the recording of the show I travelled up to Tyne Tees Television's studios in Newcastle by train the day before the recording (which was to be on Wednesday 12th July 1989) because of a train strike.

Paul B: First hosted by the much-missed TV presenter Jeremy Beadle, his You've Been Framed *days then still very-much in the future, in 1987,* Chain Letters *was another cheap and cheerful quiz show that originally was broadcast in the daytime. Subsequent hosts included Andrew O'Connor, who is now more well-known for being a creative force behind the scenes, Ted Robbins and a youthful looking Dave Spikey who would later become famous for appearing with Peter Kay on the sitcom,* Phoenix Nights. *Paul, however, took part in the quiz when it was in the safe hands of another host with the most:*

Paul W: Allan Stewart was the host and he was a really great guy. Again I wore a stupid coloured shirt at the recording because I didn't want people to miss me!

My edition of *Chain Letters* was subsequently broadcast on ITV at 9.25am on Thursday 31st May 1990. This time I actually got through to the end game and won some prize money – £630 to be exact! The next TV show I appeared on was another ITV daytime show and called *Keynotes*.

Paul B: To those of you who have little or no knowledge of daytime TV quiz and game shows circa late 1980s and early 1990s, Keynotes *was a TV quiz show that was devised for the ITV regional franchise-holder, HTV, by Reg Grundy Productions. It was broadcast on Monday to Friday mornings between 9.25am and 9.55am by a little-known presenter called Alistair Duvall in those glorious days before Jeremy Kyle settled in to the slot with his own unique brand of discussion show. There were no DNA tests in* Keynotes, *which had series on air at various times between 1989 and 1992, it was just an innocent, entertaining music quiz that helped to pass the time between* TV-am, The Time, The Place *and* Richard and Judy *hosting* This Morning.

Paul W: At the time, my knowledge of pop music was really good and everyone knew that I couldn't be beaten in a pub pop quiz so I said to Suzanne: 'I think I am going to apply for this show.'

One of the big draws for me of *Keynotes* was that you could be on TV for up to five days in a row if you won each edition! Like many shows of this type, they recorded four or five editions on the same day.

I auditioned for *Keynotes*, which was made in association with Reg Grundy Productions who were also known for being the company behind the soap opera *Neighbours* and quiz shows including *Going for Gold*, at Enterprise House in London, on Thursday 29th June 1989.

My appearance on *Keynotes* was taped in Bristol at HTV West's studios on Monday 11th September 1989. Prior to this a lady named Liz from Reg Grundy Productions called on Tuesday 25th July 1989 to tell me I had been selected to appear on the show and to ask if I would also agree to help out at their London rehearsals. This I duly did on Saturday 2nd September 1989. There were two teams on each edition of three people and the programme-makers paired me with two women.

The irony is that, given my real inability to hold a note, I had to sing on the show and sang the Cliff Richard song *Miss You Nights*.

Unfortunately my team lost on our first show and we won just £10 prize money each! However, HTV paid my travelling expenses and put me up in a hotel, so it was a good trip, although I was really disappointed not to have done better and to have been knocked out on the first show.

One of the amazing things for me about being on quiz and game shows that were made by regional television companies like HTV, TVS and Tyne Tees Television was that it gave me the opportunity to travel, at their expense, to different parts of the country that I had never been to before. This was one of the other reasons why I enjoyed the experience so much. And if they put you up in a classy hotel the night before and paid for all your meals etc. then that was even better!

Just prior to the recording of *Keynotes* in Bristol, I also unsuccessfully auditioned for *Catchphrase*, which was hosted by Roy 'Say what you see' Walker, and was made by TVS at the time in association with Action Time, and *Blackout* (*Take the Plunge*) for Thames Television. I also applied unsuccessfully for *Blankety Blank*, which was being hosted by Les Dawson at the time. However, Les and I would eventually share a studio floor together in a game show called *Fast Friends* – but more about that later!

Getting rejected to appear on quiz and game shows was always disappointing but, strangely enough, it just made me even more determined and sometimes I would even use the rejections to my advantage, as you will soon discover.

After *Keynotes* I applied unsuccessfully to Central Television in the Midlands to appear on their dart-based game, *Bullseye*, and I made a second unsuccessful bid to appear on *Catchphrase*. Again, I didn't let the knockbacks upset me and I just kept on applying for shows and, as you will see, the best was yet to come.

Chapter Five
Laughlines

By this point in my life I really had got the taste for TV fame and I was starting to think that I actually wanted to be the host of a regional TV quiz show or game show. All my friends kept saying: 'You could host a show like *Keynotes* or *Chain Letters*,' and in my mind I really was convinced at the time that I could, although, don't get me wrong, I didn't really think it would happen!

All I knew was that I wanted to go on every possible quiz show or game show that I could and on those I knew I would be suited to.

I actually revealed my desire to become the first quiz show contestant to be a host or presenter when I appeared on Jonathan Ross' Channel 4 chat show, *Tonight with Jonathan Ross*, back in 1991. In those days, however, contestants becoming presenters didn't really happen as it was in the days before reality TV started. Now, of course, former *Big Brother* housemates, such as Brian Dowling, get offered presenting work on all kinds of shows. In fact, Suzanne still says to me: 'You were just ahead of your time!'

Paul B: By now Paul had started to get column inches in his local newspapers as they printed stories about his various early game and quiz show appearances and his new-found desire to actually host such a quiz or game show. One article at the time revealed that Paul entertained the audience on one such quiz show appearance with his impersonations of Ben Elton and Cliff Richard. As photos of his appearances at the time reveal, Paul bore a striking resemblance to the said performers as well! Maybe Paul's resemblance to Elton came from the fact that he wore a specially made sparkly, Ben Elton-esque jacket which he had made at a theatrical costumiers based in Soho in London.

As if all the excitement Paul found in various TV studios across the UK wasn't memorable enough, it was also around this time that he was to find himself coming face-to-face with a member of the Royal family. Paul takes up the story of the event which has since become a treasured memory:

Paul W: A brief, but very memorable event happened in my life on Wednesday 18th October 1989. I worked for many years in a building located in Hatton Place, London, EC1. Hatton Place is a very short narrow road that runs between Hatton Wall and St Cross Street. The road is so narrow that although traffic can pass through from both ends, it is only wide enough for one lane of traffic.

I arrived at work to see some barriers being set up outside our building. I asked what was going on and was told that the barriers were for representatives of the press as Princess Diana was visiting the building opposite ours – which belonged to the ISDD (The Institute for the Study of Drug Dependency). Later that morning we could hear a lot of people gathering outside our building so my dad and I both went outside to join the crowd. It was a fine day weather-wise. The Royal car arrived and Princess Diana got out exuding her usual grace, style and elegance and met the officials from the ISDD Building and some of the people who benefited from their services.

The Princess then made her way to where both my dad and I were standing. My dad has never been a shy wallflower type of person, so he pushed his way to the front and shook hands with Princess Diana and told her how beautiful she was. I was just behind him with a camera. I was also lucky enough to shake her hand as well. She was stunning, she was delightful – I didn't want to wash my hands for a week! This was not the first time I tried to shake the hand of a Princess. A few years earlier, I was at a function where the Prince and Princess Michael of Kent were the guests of honour. I went over to the royal table with honest intentions but I soon received a tap on the shoulder from a large bodyguard and was told in no uncertain terms to get lost! Shaking hands with Princess Diana more than made up for this!

Paul B: I then asked Paul, while I chose yet another biscuit from a tin that had thoughtfully been planted in front of me, what his next TV appearance would be:

Paul W: Well, actually a man called Peter Gwyn from the BBC phoned me on Monday 23rd October 1989 to ask if I would be interested in taking part in a trial phone-in quiz on *The Noel Edmonds Saturday Roadshow* called *Poetic Justice*. This I, of course, agreed to do and the quiz took place the following day.

Because I was doing impressions of the comedian Ben Elton on the various quiz shows and game shows that I was appearing on during this period, and even used to look a bit like him especially with the aid of a Ben Elton-esque jacket that I used to wear, I was persuaded by some of my friends to apply to Susan Scott's Look-a-Like Agency. I later received a handwritten letter from the agency informing me that, at the time, there wasn't much demand for them to have a Ben Elton look-a-like on their books.

To my amazement, however, I later received a call from someone at the agency asking if I would be willing to travel down to Reading University the following day to appear as a Ben Elton look-a-like. I was informed that I would be paid the sum of £350 for my efforts. However, when I asked what I had to do, I almost fainted – they wanted me to actually perform a stand-up comedy routine as if I was Ben and not just look like him! I immediately mentioned that I wasn't a stand-up comedian and certainly didn't have any material prepared for such an appearance. I knew I would be slaughtered by the crowd if I went through with it and so I turned the offered booking down – £350 or not! My bottle well and truly went!

I was greeted on the end of my phone by the dulcet tones of one Paul O'Dell from Scottish Television on

Monday 27th November 1989. He phoned to inform me that I had been selected to appear on a show called *Laughlines*. This was a game show which was made at Scottish TV in Edinburgh for a satellite television channel called The Galaxy Channel. This was another really exciting programme to do and although Suzanne didn't appear with me on this show, she did accompany me on my trip to Edinburgh.

Six days after exchanging contracts on a new house in Elstree, the TV production company flew Suzanne and I up to Edinburgh (although I can't remember if I had to pay for her air fare or not!), and after the one hour flight we were taken to a very agreeable 4 star hotel.

I had also applied and auditioned to Action Time to appear on the game show *Win, Lose or Draw* (at the Sherlock Holmes Hotel in London) on the same day. However, *Laughlines* was the show I was chosen to appear on.

Paul B: Laughlines *was hosted by the one and only Nicholas Parsons, and was a short-lived panel game show which featured a host of then up-and-coming alternative comedians. Two lines of a limerick were provided by Parsons, and the panel each had to supply one of the three missing lines.*

I asked Paul who he remembered appearing on the panel:

Paul W: The panel on the shows I appeared on included Jo Brand, Steve Coogan, Nick Hancock, Philip Herbert (once a side-kick of Julian Clary), Bob Mills, Nick Revell and Sandi Toksvig (remember her from the classic 1980s TVS children's show, *No. 73*). All the celebrities were staying in the same hotel as us and I enjoyed chatting to each of them. Suzanne and I also shared transport with them to and from the studios.

Later, back in London, I would watch Bob Mills performing at the Comedy Store in London. He remembered me from Laughlines and we often had a chat in-between his spots. By now he had noticed me on other TV shows and he used to jokily say to me: 'You're on telly more than I am!'

Appearing on two editions of *Laughlines*, I won the first edition that I appeared on. In total I won £215 on the show and the two shows I appeared on were taped on Tuesday 13th February 1990. Again, this was another series where four to five shows were taped in a day.

Laughlines is probably the only show I have appeared on which I have never, ever, seen because I didn't have satellite television in those days and neither did anyone else we knew – how times have changed!

The quiz shows and game shows that I was by now applying for were ones that didn't require one to have much in the way of general knowledge, just requiring the contestants to have a good strong personality. I think I was ideal fodder for them and the producers knew they could have a laugh with me. I used to turn up wearing the silly jackets – and I still do to this day, as regular viewers who know me from *Big Brother's Big Mouth* will know!

Paul B: Paul then recalled to me the next game show that both he and his wife, Suzanne, appeared on together. Their appearance was not, as it turned out, the most happiest of experiences for his partner. The series in question was called Wife of the Week, *and was made by Yorkshire TV at their studios in Leeds, firstly for BSB Galaxy and later Sky 1. The show was hosted by a certain Christopher Biggins, his* I'm a Celebrity Get Me Out of Here *days still, at the time, a good seventeen years away in the future.*

Paul W: I drove both Suzanne and myself up to a hotel in Birmingham for the audition for *Wife of the Week*. At the time our daughter, Melody, was still very young so Suzanne wasn't too keen on being away from home. Suzanne and I passed the *Wife of the Week* audition and a producer called John Bartlett phoned me on Wednesday 28th February 1990 to ask us to appear on the actual show. We were told that we would be required on both Saturday 10th March and Sunday 11th March 1990 in Leeds.

Suzanne and I caught a morning train to Leeds from Kings Cross Station and later found ourselves ensconced in the Hotel Metropole, where a rehearsal for the show was held that afternoon. I was then asked to record a voiceover for the show.

The emphasis of *Wife of the Week*, as the title suggests, was not on the husband, but on the wife. There were a few Mr and Mrs-type questions at the beginning of the show and then the wives had to perform some sort of chores (imagine this show being made now in these politically-correct times!). In this case it was changing the wheel of a car and Suzanne was understandably not happy about this at all. It was a great pity because she was winning by miles up until this task. One of the other wives on the show was from Wolverhampton and was, how shall I put it, built for changing tyres so, bless her, my little Suzanne had no chance whatsoever! We didn't win that show and I think all we got was a souvenir apron.

Paul B: It was probably just as well that they didn't win as my research revealed that the weekly winners only won a rolling pin that had 'Wife of the Week' *emblazoned upon it!* Who Wants to Be a Millionaire? – *it certainly wasn't!*

Paul W: I did persuade Suzanne to appear on just one other quiz show with me after that. Fate (and Suzanne) would later decree that this would see the end of us both appearing together on the husband and wife-type shows.

On Thursday 15th March 1990 I was one of 200 studio contestants who took part in the taping of an edition of Chris Tarrant's then ITV quiz show, *Everybody's Equal*. This show, which had several similarities to the then future hit Tarrant quiz show, *Who Wants to Be a Millionaire?*, relied on audience participation using an audience voting key pad (which all of us taking part had to hand) to whittle down the contestants. One wrong answer at any stage meant that one was instantly eliminated from the show. And, yes, you guessed it, I was eliminated early on in the game. Still, I thought, 'nil desperandum'.

One day, out of the blue, I got a call from a BBC researcher (because of appearing on *Every Second Counts* I was now on a contestants' mailing list) who asked if I would like to take part in the rehearsals for a new game show called *Takeover Bid*, which was to be hosted by the legendary Bruce Forsyth. I said: 'What you mean I won't actually be on an actual edition of the show?' The researcher said: 'No, but you will be helping with the rehearsal process.' I can remember replying: 'Will Bruce Forsyth be actually there?' The researcher retorted: 'Oh yes,' so I immediately said: 'I'll do it!' After all, I was a huge fan of Brucie! To me Brucie was – and remains – King of game shows.

Paul B: Takeover Bid *would eventually be broadcast on BBC1 at various times between the 26th May 1990 and the 15th July 1991 and last a total of 28 episodes. This fun game show series was co-hosted by a very attractive ex-model called Claire Sutton who, in time, would go on to be a presenter on the satellite shopping channel, QVC.*

Paul W: The rehearsals were held at the since-demolished BBC rehearsal rooms in Acton, West London (known affectionately and ironically due to its then current state by actors, actresses, producers and director alike as the Acton Hilton). Because Bruce was going to be there I didn't have any qualms about attending. It was a brand new game show and they were basically running through ideas with me and a couple of others playing the part of contestants.

Whenever allowed, I always take my camera with me in case there is a photo opportunity. In this case I was keen, if nothing else, to get my picture taken with the legendary Bruce Forsyth that day. So after we finished the rehearsals (which we didn't get paid anything for – typical BBC!) and everyone started to leave I grabbed hold of Bruce (in the nicest possible way!) and said: 'Excuse me Bruce, would you mind if I had my photo taken with you?' He replied, 'No, of course!' So I got someone else to take our photo together and that was a real thrill for me!

Regrettably, I missed out meeting the then future *Strictly Come Dancing* host again after I failed to make it onto *The Generation Game*. Forsyth was hosting a new run of the *Gen. Game* and I, along with Suzanne's aunty Renee (who was the only one willing to audition with me!) unsuccessfully auditioned for the game show on Friday 24th August 1990.

I then appeared on another satellite TV show made for BSB. This time, however, it was a chat show hosted by Mike Smith. This went by the imaginative title of *The Mike Smith Show*. Again, I didn't get paid for appearing on the show but it was great fun to take part in. They were looking for people to take part in a discussion who had appeared on TV game shows and by now I certainly fitted that description!

At the time the game shows I was applying for, but not getting, included, *Cannon & Ball's Casino*, a game show made by Yorkshire TV in association with Action Time, which I auditioned for at the University Arms Hotel in Cambridge.

Paul B: Sky decided to resurrect the classic ITV quiz show, The Sale of the Century, *in the early 1990s. Originally hosted by Nicholas Parsons, and made by Anglia Television, the quiz used to start each week with the much-remembered introduction given by John Benson of: 'And now, from Norwich, it's the quiz of the week.' Sky's version, however, was hosted by a man called Peter Marshall and made at what was then LWT's South Bank studios in London.*

By Paul's own admission, his general knowledge wasn't his best asset. The types of quiz shows and game shows that he usually applied for were the type of ones that required contestants to be entertaining, to have a good personality and very good sense of humour. So, I then asked Paul what had made him decide to apply to take part in the new version of Sale of the Century:

Paul W: Well, although I knew I wasn't going to be very good on this show because of my lack of general knowledge, it was one of those quiz shows that was shown daily and needed a great deal of contestants to take part. So I thought: 'I am going to have a go.'

I filled in yet another application form and went along and attended an audition. As it turned out I just got enough questions right to pass the audition and to be invited to take part in the show.

The edition of *Sale of the Century* which I took part in was one of several taped on Thursday 6th September 1990. The show was later broadcast by Sky 1 on the 18th December 1990. I was the first to be knocked out of the show and received a consolation prize of The Times Concise Atlas of the World. Still, it made a change from a clock or a mug!

Incidentally, fans of *The X-Factor* and *Britain's Got Talent* might be interested to know that a certain Simon Cowell appeared on the same series of *Sale of the Century* as I did! So obviously Cowell was working on his own quest for TV fame via the quiz show circuit in those days!

Cowell, who was 30 at the time, didn't win the Fiat Uno he played for on *Sale of the Century,* but, as a Sun newspaper article revealed some years later, he did win a £20 set of kitchen utensils! Simon's quest for TV fame has, of course, been slightly more successful than mine!

But one of the most embarrassing experiences I have had during my quest for TV fame – which I didn't know if I should recall as it still makes me quiver with nerves even now – was an audition to appear on the second series of *Stars in Their Eyes*, which in those days was being hosted by another much-missed TV personality, Leslie Crowther.

On Tuesday 5th December 1989 I applied for an audition for *Stars in Their Eyes;* and the following day I was phoned by a lady named Adele Emm at Granada TV to say that an audition time had been set for me on Sunday 17th December 1989.

Despite the fact that I couldn't sing I had become so obsessed with appearing on TV I just felt I had to apply for *Stars in Their Eyes.* As it turned out it was the most nerve-racking thing I have ever done! I auditioned as – wait for it – Cliff Richard. And if I wasn't making things hard enough for myself I selected to sing possibly the hardest song I could have chosen – *Miss You Nights*.

I had a friend called Mandy Rubinstein who unfortunately died at a very young age of cancer. She was a very talented singer who had made an appearance on a Sky talent show hosted by Keith Chegwin called *Sky Star Search*. She was an accomplished singer and piano player and I can remember seeing her at a friend's party. She was a lovely girl with a great personality and I said to her: 'You're not going to believe this, but I'm going to audition for *Stars in Their Eyes.'* I continued: 'You couldn't give me a couple of singing lessons could you?' Fortunately she said 'Yes'. I later went over to her house and we went through the song *Miss You Nights* a few times but despite this I wasn't proving to be Cliff Richard-standard, shall we say.

Ever the optimist, I attended my audition which was being held at the Granada Rehearsal Rooms, 2–3 Brixton Road, Kennington, London, SW9. I found myself in this room and, just like you see on shows now like *The X-Factor*, there was a table with a panel of judges sitting behind ready to audition me. They were very friendly, however, and I started to go through the song accompanied by a professional pianist. But even as I sang I knew instantly that I was badly out of tune. Alas! my dream to appear on *Stars in Their Eyes* died there and then in that cold and dusty rehearsal room. This was a fact that was later confirmed for me in a standard issue letter sent to all those would-be *Stars in Their Eyes* contestants which I received from Jane Macnaught, the shows producer.

Paul B: But Paul's quest for TV fame obviously didn't stop in that rehearsal room in Kennington, London. Getting back to what he knew best Paul found himself appearing on a quiz show with Suzanne called All Clued Up. *The series was made by TVS and ran on the ITV network at various times, including a Sunday afternoon slot, from April 1988 to August 1991. David 'Diddy' Hamilton hosted the show. According to Paul's wife, Suzanne, the set was designed so that the contestants were lower than 'Diddy' so that they did not appear taller than he was!*

Paul W: Appearing on *All Clued Up* was very enjoyable. It was recorded at the Southampton studios of the then ITV southern franchise-holders', TVS, with all of our expenses paid for. This has to date, however, been the last quiz or game show that Suzanne has appeared on with me – as I messed up the questions yet again!

There was a great camaraderie between all of the contestants on *All Clued Up* and we all stayed in the same hotel and had a drink at the bar together the night before. One of the most enjoyable parts of appearing on this and other such shows is the people, as they tend to be like-minded so it makes it easier for one to strike up a conversation.

When it came to the recording of our edition of *All Clued Up* we won a cash prize of £450! Although Suzanne, not surprisingly, won most of the money for us – a fact that, quite-rightly, she will never ever let me forget!

Chapter Six
Beating the Ban

Paul B: The James Whale Radio Show *was a late night show broadcast on ITV1 in the days when it was just known as ITV. It used to go out live in the early hours of a Saturday morning and was ideal post-pub closing television for viewers who had downed one or two pints! It was harmless fun and was presented, as the title suggests, by radio DJ, James Whale. Calling the programme* The James Whale Radio Show *was obviously an ironic title and the show itself was broadcast live on television from the reception area (which was turned into a mock TV studio each Friday) at Yorkshire TV's studios in Leeds.*

It was at the start of 1991 that Paul received a call asking him if he would be interested in appearing on the programme. Paul takes up the story:

Paul W: I had a phone call from the producer of *Wife of the Week* which, as you may remember, was a game show that Suzanne and I appeared on and was also made by Yorkshire TV. The producer in question and I had got chatting when we were up at Yorkshire TV and he had obviously kept me in mind. On this occasion he asked if I would be interested in taking part with a friend in a spoof game show slot which was to take part in an edition of *The James Whale Radio Show*. I immediately agreed to his request.

Before we knew it my friend David Phillips and I found ourselves on a train bound for Leeds. Yorkshire TV had agreed to pay all of our expenses and arranged for us to stay in a nice hotel in Leeds. We were picked up by a car from the hotel and taken to the since decommissioned studios in Leeds, which had played host over the years to programmes such as the soap, *Emmerdale*, the Leonard Rossiter sitcom, *Rising Damp*, the game show, *3-2-1* and the Keith Barron and Gwen Taylor sitcom, *Duty Free*.

Just a short walk from the studio where the long-running Channel 4 quiz show, *Countdown*, was based, was Yorkshire TV's reception. It was here that we found a busy team preparing for that night's show.

The spoof game show we were to take part in included a karaoke round. This might not sound that exciting, but back then karaoke was new to the UK so it was quite a novelty. In the event, I can recall singing the Jerry Lee Lewis song, *Great Balls Of Fire*. There was also a round that involved the contestants to take part in a strip-tease if they got the answers wrong. I can remember that my friend David got down to his underpants, but fortunately for the viewers I didn't have to take off as many of my clothes! It was all great fun and the show was very laid back.

Later, following photos with James Whale, who we found to be a very affable guy, David and I were both given our reward each for taking part in the show. So what was it – I hear you cry – that we received? Well, it wasn't a cash prize or a holiday for two in Barbados, Oh no. We received a *James Whale Radio Show* t-shirt and a packet of condoms each!

Paul B: Up until this point, despite not getting onto every quiz show and game show that he applied to, Paul was being asked to fill out many, many application forms and invited to attend auditions for such shows being made by the production company called Action Time. But suddenly his phone had fallen silent and postal replies to his applications stopped. So, I asked Paul, what had suddenly gone wrong:

Paul W: I wasn't quite sure. So in view of this I sent the following letter to Action Time's Manchester base on 18th February 1991 to ask if there was a problem with my recent applications and to see if I had, as I suspected, been 'blacklisted':

Dear Malcolm,

In my quest to appear on as many game shows as possible, I am writing to find out if I have been forgotten by Action Time, as I have not been offered an audition of any kind for nearly a year.

Two weeks ago I appeared on the Yorkshire TV programme *The James Whale Radio Show* in a game show send-up to end all send-ups! It even made *Remote Control* look like a straight game show! After that appearance I am ready for anything!

Could you please let me know if I have been 'blacklisted' by Action Time? Or if my new address (above) is not on file?

Thank you.

Yours sincerely

Paul Wilder – Mr Game Show

Note that I had the cheek to sign off the letter as 'Mr Game Show'! This was a term being used by my local press! I soon received a prompt reply letter dated 19th February 1991 from Malcolm Quiggin, the then head of production at Action Time, who confirmed my suspicions:

Dear Paul,

Many thanks for your letter. I am afraid you are a victim of your own success. You certainly have been 'blacklisted' by Action Time because we are always looking for new and exciting contestants to give them a chance of appearing on TV. I know you will want to give them the same opportunities that you have.

It may be unknown to you, but *Lucky Ladders* and *All Clued Up* are both owned by Action Time, but licensed to broadcasters to make, so you have indirectly been on two of our shows recently.

Yours sincerely

Malcolm Quiggin
Head of Production
Action Time

You will notice that the letter mentions my appearance on *Lucky Ladders*. The show, which was hosted by Lennie Bennett, was taped on Monday 12th November 1990 at Anglia Television's then studio complex in Norwich, where the original *Sale of the Century* had been made with Nicholas Parsons at the helm.

I appeared on this show once again with my friend David Phillips, who had appeared with me on the spoof game show on *The James Whale Radio Show*. We didn't do very well on this show and I remember it being quite a difficult game. In the end we both won a consolation prize each of a *Lucky Ladders* mug and watch – which I still have to this day.

Ironically, as these lines were being typed, both Paul Burton and I heard the sad news that Lennie Bennett had passed away. I actually saw Lennie performing live in a summer season show in Great Yarmouth the year I travelled up there to see The Krankies. He was appearing on a different show with Freddie Starr, who was topping the bill. Bennett closed the first half of the show and had the audience in stitches. He was a very funny and underrated comedian. At *Lucky Ladders* he was also very warm with the contestants and seemed a genuinely friendly guy.

Returning to the letter, you may have thought that I would have been upset by this and have viewed it as a frustrating knock back. On the contrary, I thought the letter was perfect for my cause and I immediately started to think of ways that I could use this in my quest for TV fame and the associated publicity that could come along with it.

The next TV programme I appeared on was a short-lived Saturday night game show broadcast on BBC1 called *Fast Friends*. This was hosted by the legendary and much-missed comedian and writer, Les Dawson. I remember at the time thinking that Les didn't look too well and, sadly, he passed away just a couple of years later. *Fast Friends* was taped at BBC Elstree, on Clarendon Road in Borehamwood, Hertfordshire, situated close to Elstree Studios and very close to where we lived at the time in Elstree itself. Okay, geography lesson over!

Despite having filled in an application form and been accepted to take part in *Fast Friends*, I, like other contestants on the show were not guaranteed a place. In the first part of each edition of the show Dawson would ask questions to members of the audience – all of whom had applied to appear on the show. Those who Les chose to answer the questions and gave a correct reply would be chosen to join a team of four up on stage.

When the chance to answer a question came I jumped up out of my seat and put my right hand up as far as I could. Les chose me and fortunately I answered the easy question correctly, so before I knew it, I was up on the stage!

Let me just go back a little and remind you that I had been officially 'blacklisted' by Action Time. Well, Action Time was involved in the making of *Fast Friends* for the BBC! So to get through the application process (I wasn't going to be beaten by a blacklisting ban!) I used the name Gary Keyes, which is my brother-in-laws name. No audition was required, but in the hope that I wouldn't be recognised at the studios on the day by any of the representatives of Action Time, I gelled back my hair and took my glasses off. In the event it worked and the team I was part of went on to win the show and each of us received a colour pocket TV and a *Fast Friends* address book! It was a fantastic feeling to have beaten the ban.

However, the pocket TV didn't work very well so, now it is many years ago, I can reveal that I cheekily took it to a high street store and exchanged it for cash – £145.00 to be exact! I remember thinking how pleased I was about this although, of course, I was more over the moon about the fact that I had managed to appear on a Saturday night primetime television show on BBC1.

Both transmission dates and times for the editions of *Fast Friends* and *Lucky Ladders*, as it turned out, were scheduled to be within days of each other. *Fast Friends* was scheduled to be broadcast on BBC1 on Saturday 6th April 1991 and *Lucky Ladders* on ITV on Wednesday 10th April 1991. And, as I had been banned from appearing on game shows and quiz shows made by Action Time, I thought to myself: 'There's a story here that might interest a newspaper.' I had, after all, fooled Action Time and got to appear on *Fast Friends* – and was part of the winning team! So I decided to ring up The Sun newspaper to whom I said: 'I don't know if you are interested, but I have it in writing that I have actually been blacklisted by Action Time from appearing on the TV quiz shows and game shows that they make for broadcasters. However, I recently disguised myself, gave myself a false name and managed to appear on Les Dawson's BBC1 Saturday night show called *Fast Friends.'*

The reporter who I spoke to loved the story and said he would get someone at the paper to ring me back to discuss the possible story further. A man named Jim Taylor then called back, interviewed me on the phone and then arranged for a photographer to come over to my house, which he duly did, to take a photo of me next to a shot of myself on TV in *Fast Friends.*

Suzanne and I visited friends on Sunday 7th April 1991. By this point I had been told by Jim Taylor at The Sun that my story was set to be included in Monday's edition of the paper. I had, of course, told Suzanne, and we decided not to tell anybody in case the story didn't make it into the paper. How I managed not to tell our friends that night I don't know! I was really excited at the prospect that my photo and a story about me may be appearing in a national newspaper the next day.

I had discovered that if you went to a London railway station such as Kings Cross very late at night, or very early in the morning, whichever way you want to look at it, that you could buy copies of the following morning's national papers. So as Suzanne and I clambered into our car after leaving our friends' house at about midnight, I turned to her and said: 'I want to drive up to London to try and get a copy of the paper from Kings Cross Station.' Suzanne agreed to come with me so I nervously drove to the aforementioned station. After buying a copy of the tabloid in question I opened the paper and there on page 3 was the report about me together with a photo! The headline screamed:

'I PULLED A FAST ONE ON TV LES'
Paul's disguise beats quiz show ban

I couldn't believe it! I rushed back to the car and excitedly showed the paper to Suzanne. I didn't get much in the way of sleep that night as I was simply too excited.

I was back in the office by 8 o'clock the following morning but my mind was not focused on the idea of working. Just when I was starting to try and get my head together to do a days work the phone began to ring. Then it rang again and again and again. By now friends and relatives had seen the article in The Sun while eating their cornflakes.

A phone call actually came from Radio 1. The radio station had also spotted the report in the paper and wanted to cover the story on *Newsbeat*. I then received a call from British Forces Radio and then Capital Radio in London, both wanting to interview me. Suddenly my fun quest for TV fame was becoming newsworthy!

Don't get me wrong, I was under no illusions, I knew I was the light-hearted story, the light relief in that day's news but I was more than happy with that! I hoped it would help put a smile on one or two people's faces at a time when the country was yet again going through a miserable recession.

Just when I thought the phone was finally going to stop ringing I got a call from someone at The Daily Mirror newspaper. The paper had also seen the article in The Sun and wanted to do a proper feature on me! They liked the fact that I had used a disguise to cheekily get on *Fast Friends* and wanted to add photos of me in various guises as part of the feature.

I went to a meeting with Alec Lom from The Daily Mirror at a pub which was situated opposite what was then the offices of the paper. We discussed the feature and he informed me that he intended to book studio time and a professional make-up artist for the photos that would be part of the spread in the paper.

On the day of the photo shoot for the feature I went to the offices of The Daily Mirror, which at the time were not far from where I worked. They showed me around the offices and then took me to a studio where I was worked on by a make-up artist. I had a great time being made up to be a punk rocker with dyed spiky hair. They also turned me into an old man by making my hair grey and giving me a moustache. Finally they put a bald wig on my head and the end results looked hilarious! This was a brilliant double page colour feature.

When the feature finally appeared in The Daily Mirror's TV Weekly dated 27th April–3rd May 1991, the headlines in the article read:

Meet the game show addict who just can't be stopped from appearing on screen.
Banned ... but not beaten

The feature included Alex Lom's interview with me, professional photos by Nigel Wright and photos of me from my personal collection with Nicholas Parsons, Paul Daniels and Bruce Forsyth. The spread also mentioned my desire and dream to become a quiz show or a game show host.

I then decided to try and push my fifteen minutes of fame even further by persuading my better half, Suzanne, to ring up Channel X, the makers of *Tonight with Jonathan Ross*, to see if they would be interested in including me as a guest on their show. Was I now being too ambitious? Maybe – but it worked! To my amazement I was duly booked for an appearance on Jonathan's show in order to discuss my recent ban and all of my various quiz show and game show appearances.

Chapter Seven
Tonight With Jonathan Ross

Having expressed an interest in my recent newspaper coverage, my various quiz show and game show appearances and the now infamous ban, a representative from Channel X invited me to a meeting at their offices off Tottenham Court Road in London. I attended the meeting and was interviewed by a very pleasant female researcher. I think they wanted to see if I would be capable of being interviewed on the show. The researcher seemed happy and informed me that she would need to talk to Jonathan Ross, and that they would call me in the next few days.

Having waited patiently for a call back from the researcher, I decided to risk seeming like a pest and I rang her back. She informed me that the situation was looking good and that they were now looking at finding a date for me to appear on the show.

A short while later the same researcher called me back again and asked if I would be willing to appear on the show on Monday 22nd April 1991. Would I? Of course I agreed to appear on the show immediately. The researcher ran through a few details regarding the show. She asked if I would be willing to bring along some of the prizes (or consolation prizes) that I had been given during my various quiz and game show appearances. She also confirmed that Channel X would pay me the standard appearance fee of £150! It all seemed like some kind of a wonderful dream!

On hearing of my upcoming appearance on Jonathan's Channel 4 series, some of my friends and relatives started to express concerns as to whether I would be okay on the show. They feared that I would end up looking like a laughing stock and that Jonathan would tear me to shreds during the interview. I must admit that I was a little worried but that I wasn't going to let this put me off this golden opportunity. After all, I reasoned, this might be the best piece of TV exposure I may ever get!

Come the day of the show, Channel X sent a car to pick Suzanne and I up in order to take us to Riverside Studios in Hammersmith, where *Tonight with Jonathan Ross* was being made and broadcast from. All of the production team on the show were very friendly and once I had been introduced to them a runner showed me to my dressing room – I felt like a real star!

Later, Jonathan Ross came into my dressing room to introduce himself. He shook hands and we then sat down to have a brief chat before taking me down onto the set in the studio and allowing me to sit down in the guests chair in order to get a 'feel for it'. Finally back to the Green Room where the other guest on that edition of the show, author Kitty Kelley, was relaxing.

In the foyer, where the audience queued prior to entering the studio, was a blackboard (no expense spared!) which featured the names of the shows guests. It was a great thrill to see my name on the board along with that of author Kitty Kelley. Kelley is an American author who made her name writing controversial biographies of the likes of: Jacqueline Onassis, Elizabeth Taylor and Frank Sinatra. On this occasion she was appearing on Jonathan's show to promote her latest book: *Nancy Regan – The Unauthorized Biography*.

On arriving back in the Green Room I was introduced to Kitty. I was already wearing my sparkly 'star' suit ready for the show and Kelley obviously thought I was some kind of a 'real' celebrity and we chatted and got on famously – if you pardon the pun!

I told Kitty that my mum was a big fan of her books and that I had bought a copy of her latest book as a birthday present for her. Of course, when I asked Kelley to sign it she was delighted. The message she wrote was:

To Gloria,

This is a special gift from your highly talented son, Paul, and we both hope it gives you a great read.

Have a wonderful birthday and may your glass be as full as Nancy's!

Best
Kitty Kelley

All guests were asked to sign a large message board with a permanent marker pen. These were later auctioned off at a later date for charity. Kitty Kelley signed and then I wrote a message that read:

> The most exciting day of my life.
> Paul Wilder

For a short time I really felt what it was like to be a 'celebrity'.

Paul B: I then suggested that Paul and I actually watch a video recording of the said show. Paul agreed that this was a good idea and we adjourned to watch the show.

Paul then admitted to still feeling nervous of watching the programme, even though he had viewed it many times. It was almost as if the nerves he had experienced before taking part in the show some 18 years before (at the time of our interview) had returned.

The TV sprang into life and we were faced with the sight of the much-loved entertainer Paul O'Grady hosting his popular teatime chat show.

With the video now rolling, we were instantly taken back the best part of 18 years as the opening title sequence for Tonight with Jonathan Ross *played. I well-remember watching and enjoying this series back in the early 1990s. It was a more genteel version of his present Friday night chat show for obvious reasons, not least because the earlier version was broadcast at*

6.30pm in the evening. But it was still similar in many ways, although it was broadcast live.

Ross walked out and was greeted with a warm reception from the crowd. He then launched into the type of witty, impressive and slickly delivered monologue that fans, including myself, of Jonathan's have come to know, love and expect.

With the opening monologue, which included the recent London Marathon as its subject matter, over, it was time for a youthful looking Ross to introduce a certain Paul Wilder to the assembled studio audience and the TV viewers. Paul had been asked to sit in the audience and to enter on cue as if making a Price is Right *contestant-style entrance. This he did at exactly 6.33pm clutching a bag of various souvenirs from the quiz and game show appearances he had made to date.*

Paul's friends and relatives need not have worried about his ability to hold his own during the interview. The ensuing interview saw Ross and Wilder engaging in friendly and entertaining banter about Paul's quest for TV fame and his various appearances. A seemingly unsure audience soon began to warm to Paul; although both Jonathan and I were in total agreement that his Ben Elton impression should have scored more of a hit with the assembled crowd.

Producing the likes of his Every Second Counts *clock, recalling the story of how events had led him to being 'blacklisted' by Action Time and speaking of his dream to become a TV host well-and-truly filled the allotted eight minutes of air time Paul was given. With every one of his £150 earned, Paul was thanked by Ross and given an enthusiastic cheer by the audience present.*

With the programme viewing over, Paul seemed to visibly relax. We discussed the show as we moved back to our now familiar interview space in the dining room and the temporarily stopped tape recorder was then moved from alongside the TV set, plugged in once more and the tape restarted. So, with his impressive Tonight with Jonathan Ross *appearance made, I was eager to find out what came next for Paul:*

Paul W: Looking back, to be paid to appear as a guest on Jonathan Ross's chat show has been one of the biggest highlights of my TV appearances so far. It also gave me a real thrill to see my name mentioned in the various TV listings pages for the programme.

After the programme I decided to send out about 12 video tapes to various broadcasters and production companies who made quiz shows and game shows in the hope that I might be able to audition for them for various presenting roles. Unfortunately, despite receiving several really polite and positive letters back from them, no formal offers of auditions came.

I was ahead of my time, there were no reality TV stars in those days and all quiz shows and game shows were being mainly presented by experienced professional performers and celebrities. The days of reality TV stars being given opportunities for hosting shows were well and truly in the future at the time. I think maybe I should have sent out many more letters in an attempt to score TV hosting opportunities, but at the time we had a young daughter and I was helping to run a busy family business so this was simply out of the question.

By now, because of the ban by Action Time, having appeared on several quiz shows and game shows, and almost exhausted the possibilities to audition for other shows, I decided to call it a day. I thought to myself: 'I've had a great time but I've gone as far as I can.' I decided it was time to move on and concentrate all my energies on my marriage, my daughter and my work.

Paul B: I then asked if it bothered Paul, and did it make him feel jealous, when he saw other people appearing on quiz shows and game shows during his 'TV retirement':

Paul W: No, I just thought: I've been there, seen it and done it! I did feel a little jealous, though, when *Who Wants to Be a Millionaire?* came along and I saw people winning huge pots of cash. But I soon got over it. I thought: 'I've had my 15 minutes of fame and just got on with other stuff in my busy life.'

I must admit that I did ring up *Who Wants to Be a Millionaire?* a few times when it first started. But I have never been a fan of having to pay for premium rate phone calls in order to apply to be on a show. It was almost like taking part in a lottery. My personal preference and knack for getting on shows was where you sent off for an application form, filled it out and added some funny stories to get the attention of producers and researchers, such as the one about accidentally spilling red wine down my wife's dress at our wedding. Then I used to like to go along to the auditions and relished the opportunity to display my personality.

Paul B: I then went on to ask Paul if he has ever thought of applying and auditioning for Big Brother*:*

Paul W: All my family and friends were constantly asking that, but I never liked the idea of being in the house away or being locked away from them and the outside world for any amount of time. Besides, I would probably be evicted first! Although, as I will mention later, I became a regular member of the *Big Brother*-related spin off discussion show *Big Brother's Big Mouth*, as I am such a huge *Big Brother* fan.

So for the best part of nine years life continued as it had before, and I contented myself with the fact that I had experienced the world of television and my time in the spotlight climaxing in a very enjoyable appearance on *Tonight with Jonathan Ross*. My wife and daughter had got my full attention again and Suzanne in particular was probably relieved that I had put my desire for TV fame in the past.

Paul B: So, I wondered, what was life like in the Wilder household during Paul's temporary retirement from TV? What did the family do with Paul's quest for TV fame now in the past? Melody, Paul's daughter, recalled to me a particular birthday that has stayed in her memory from this time:

Melody: Mum and Dad arranged a party for my seventh birthday. All my friends from school were invited and a disco and clown had been arranged for entertainment. On the day of my party, I went down with chicken pox and really didn't enjoy the party. I have hated clowns ever since but it has not put me off partying – although my kind of partying is now of the clubbing variety! I can remember some really great holidays as I grew up. I think I was aged 7 when we all travelled to Disneyland in Florida.

After a day at Universal Studios we went back to the car park and couldn't find the car. Dad had forgotten exactly where he parked. What made it worse was that the heavens opened and we were looking around this massive car park in a tropical storm. All we knew was that we were looking for a red car – but there were thousands of red cars! Mum was understandably not best pleased and a lot of shouting was going on! It must have taken a whole hour to find the car, by which time we were wetter than if we had jumped in the pool with Shamu the whale at Sea World! When we got back to the hotel and dried off we all saw the funny side of it.

A couple of years later we went to the west coast of America. Looking back, it was a really great holiday, but I can remember being really bored as dad drove the famous drive from San Francisco to Los Angeles. I think he got really fed up of me saying 'Are we there yet?'

On the same trip we went to Las Vegas and stayed at the MGM Grand Hotel. I remember as we stopped in the casino bit, we were moved on immediately as children aren't allowed in the casino. There was however, a fun fair at the hotel and dad and I won loads of teddy bears. When we got back to Heathrow, one of our cases didn't arrive. It was the one with all the teddy bears in! I was so upset. Luckily the case in question was found and delivered to our house just a few days later.

Paul W: The years that followed my appearance on *Tonight with Jonathan Ross* were filled with more hobbies and pastimes. I took up tenpin bowling and joined a league, partnered with my chum David Phillips, who had originally appeared with me on *The James Whale Radio Show*. Initially we played at North Harrow Bowl, which doesn't sound very glamorous, but on one night a bunch of famous comedians turned up to bowl. I think it was Lenny Henry or Harry Enfield's stag night. I saw them from a distance but it would have been extremely uncool to leave my league to go over to them. I believe Ben Elton might have even been there but I didn't see him. We still play for a league in Dunstable, my scratch average is 170, but we usually end up in the bottom few places in the results table!

I am always committed (and some say I should be!) to whatever I am doing but as I always said about my game show appearances: 'It's the taking part that counts.' However, as footballers might say, 'I give everything I try my best shot!'

Starting a fantasy football league which, at its peak, had 73 people taking part, I compiled and printed a newsletter once a month that contained the league table and reports on the movers and shakers in it. At the end of each season I would arrange an annual presentation night at The Orange Tree pub in Totteridge. As the evening went on this would admittedly descend into a regular p**s-up!

On a couple of occasions we went to the Daily Telegraph Fantasy Football Awards Dinner at a London hotel. These were always fun evenings and gave us a chance to meet some football legends including: Sir Bobby Charlton, Pat Jennings and David Seaman, to name but a few.

Another football dinner that we went to was the testimonial evening for England and Arsenal's physio, Fred Street. There was a great turn out of stars for this occasion. The 1966 World Cup hero Sir Geoff Hurst was there and Walkers' Crisps man, Gary Lineker. These evenings present great opportunities for chatting to some of your heroes, not forgetting some great photo opportunities. It was also on one such occasion that I met the delightful *Birds of a Feather* actress and Arsenal fan, Pauline Quirke.

Mentioning some of my football heroes, reminds me that during the time in the 1960s when my dad had a little shop in Hatton Garden that sold watches, some quite famous footballers often visited to buy watches. These included: Arsenal's Frank McLintock, George Graham and even the late, great, Bobby Moore.

In 1969, Arsenal reached the *League Cup Final*. My dad came home from work one day and said that Arsenal star George Graham was getting us tickets for the Final! We were going to collect them personally from George's house in Southgate. I was so excited! Here was I a 14-year-old Arsenal fan going to meet one of his heroes! On the day we visited George he welcomed us into his home and gave my dad tickets for the Final and gave me a black and white photo, which he autographed. I thanked him but I was too star-struck to say anything else!

On Saturday 15th March 1969 we went to the *League Cup Final*, at the original twin-towered Wembley Stadium. The match, however, did not go to plan.

Indeed, it turned out to be one of the biggest cup shocks in football history. Arsenal were riding high in the then First Division while Swindon Town were in the Third Division. I can't bring myself to go into too much detail but the match went to extra time after the teams were drawing 1–1. Arsenal were then expected to win comfortably, but Swindon's winger Don Rogers scored twice for them to win the cup. I am not afraid to say that I was in tears. Despite the disappointing result, I had met my first football star in 'real life' as we used to say.

I have mentioned that my dad's story was published in a book called *The Boy's* by Martin Gilbert. Martin is a historian and has written several books on the holocaust. He has known my dad for several years. One day in 1996 my dad received a phone call from Martin to ask if he was going to see comedian Jackie Mason's show at the London Palladium. My parents were going and so Martin explained to my dad that he had met Mason in New York a couple of weeks previously where they had discussed Martin's book. They had arranged that when Jackie came over to perform his show at the London Palladium that they would meet up again and Martin would give him a copy of his book.

On the night of the show, Martin, due to unforeseen circumstances, could not attend the show, so he asked my dad if he would take the signed copy backstage and present it to Jackie. After the show, my parents went backstage but Mason, who was wearing his overcoat, brushed past them in the corridor and seemed to be in a bit of a hurry. Dad explained that he had brought a copy of the book *The Boys* for him, as arranged with the author. Jackie, who indeed confirmed that he was in a rush, then invited mum and dad to join him for tea at the Dorchester Hotel (where he was staying) the following day.

I then received a call from my dad who asked if I would like to meet Jackie Mason. 'Of course,' I replied. So on the Sunday, Suzanne and I took my parents up to the Dorchester Hotel to meet the great man in person.

We arrived at the hotel and informed the receptionist why we were there. The said receptionist duly paged his room but there was no reply. She was really helpful and tried very hard to contact Jackie, but alas there was no joy.

Leaving the book at reception I then wrote a note to Jackie explaining how disappointed my dad was that he had not shown up for the pre-arranged tea. I wrote my dad's address and telephone number thinking that the comedian might at least send a thank you note and an apology.

Back at work on the Monday afternoon the phone in my office was answered by Kim, one of my assistants. I heard her say: 'No, Mr Wilder Snr is not here at the moment,' and then put the phone down. As it happened, my dad was in his office on the floor above, but Kim had not bothered to ask. I asked Kim who was on the phone and she replied: 'Someone called Jackie Mason.' I screamed: 'What? You are joking? Don't you know who Jackie Mason is?' Kim shook her head and said: 'No, who's Jackie Mason?' My other assistants – Carol, Pat and Sally – all started to laugh, they certainly knew!

I quickly phoned back the Dorchester and they put me through to the comedian's PA. He then put Jackie on the phone to my dad. He apologised for not being at the hotel on Sunday and thanked my dad for the book, which he had already started reading, and was finding very moving. By way of a thank you, Mason invited my dad to join him for lunch the following Wednesday. My dad took him up on the offer and they dined at the appropriately named Fortnum and Mason's restaurant in Piccadilly.

Four years later, in 2000, my daughter, Melody, became the person to finally re-ignite my passion and desire for appearing on television.

My quest and my desire for TV fame were both back and this time even stronger than before. I didn't know what opportunities I would find, after all, television had changed quite a bit since I had appeared on Jonathan Ross' show back in 1991. But I just knew it was time to see if I still had the ability to charm my way onto TV shows again, by filling in application forms and attending auditions, which both gave me the opportunity to let my personality shine.

I'd had a great deal of fun appearing on TV before and I sincerely hoped that there would be more fun and laughter to be found. What fate had in store for me, I was just going to have to be patient and wait and see.

Chapter Eight
On The TV Comeback Trail

Melody, who was about 13 years old at the time, happened to see an advert in the London Evening Standard for a new game show that was looking for contestants. While I had dismissed the idea of applying for such shows in the last nine years, for some reason I decided that I would make the effort and apply for this show.

Paul B: During the process of writing this book I decided to ask Melody whether she watched any of the video recordings of her dad's various early TV appearances when she was growing up:

Melody: Not really, but I can remember being shown the Daily Mirror feature on dad and thinking it was really weird that there was photos of my dad in the paper dressed as both a 'bald' and an 'old' man.

Paul B: I then asked Melody what was the first actual TV appearance of her dad's that she can actually remember watching:

Melody: I think it was when he appeared on Wheel of Fortune. *This was on at about five-thirty in the afternoon and mum always watched it. I thought it was really funny when dad was on it!*

Paul B: But we are getting ahead of ourselves, Paul was just describing how he came to find himself back in the limelight once again:

Paul W: The show in question turned out to be *It's Anybody's Guess*, a daytime show made for ITV1 and hosted by Paul Ross. How ironic, I thought, my previous TV appearance, which I had started to think was to be my last, was with Jonathan Ross. Now here I was being asked, following an audition, to appear with his brother, Paul, on his show. To add to the coincidences the production company making the show was run by Simon Ross, who was another of the Ross clan! It's a small world!

Having been accepted to appear, I made my way to what is now known as Cactus TV's studios in South London. Paul Ross and the whole production team were all really amiable and made me feel very welcome. Already the whole feeling was back as we entered the studio and I soon realised just how much I had missed appearing on television and everything that was involved with it.

One of the reasons I most enjoyed appearing on *It's Anybody's Guess* was because members of the public were paired with celebrities. They paired me with an actress called Joy Brook, who at the time was playing DC Kerry Homes in one of my favourite TV shows,

The Bill, so I was thrilled. Brook, incidentally, went on to appear in the Ben Elton sitcom on BBC1 called *The Thin Blue Line*, which starred Rowan Atkinson.

Actor Ross Davidson, who was best-known for having played Andy O'Brien in the BBC soap *EastEnders*, was also on the show. Sadly, Ross was to die from a brain tumour at the age of 56 in 2006. Davidson was a very friendly actor and I was upset when I heard that he had passed away.

I didn't win my edition of *It's Anybody's Guess,* but by now I had been bitten by the bug again and travelling back home to Elstree, with my consolation prize t-shirt, I decided that I would start applying to appear on shows again and see what happened.

Paul B: So thanks to his daughter Melody, Paul's quest for TV fame began once again. I then asked which show/s he applied for and appeared on next:

Paul W: Well, after a failed audition to take part in *The Weakest Link*, on the 22nd June 2000, I decided to apply for the BBC1 daytime quiz show, *Wipeout*.

When the application for *Wipeout* arrived in the post my heart sank – it was from Action Time. As you may remember, the aforementioned production company had banned me from appearing on shows they made back in 1991. I wasn't sure if this ban was still in operation or whether details of this ban were still against my name on their database, so I decided to take a risk and apply – only with a different name! So when I filled in the application form I used my full name – Leon Paul Wilder. That way I thought if I am accepted onto the show and I win any cash prize they can make out the cheque payable to this name and I will still be able to cash it, after all this full version of my name is on my bank account! By now we had also moved to a different address in Elstree which I also hoped would fool them!

When I completed the application form I tried to keep as much information back as possible about all of my previous extensive game and quiz show appearances in case they rejected me! To my surprise, however, I received an invitation to attend an audition for *Wipeout* on Monday 24th July 2000 at 1, Heathcote Court, London, which I duly attended. I passed my audition for *Wipeout* and on a subsequently arranged date I travelled up to Manchester and found myself staying in yet another comfortable hotel.

The edition of *Wipeout* that I was scheduled to appear on was one of four or five being recorded the next day.

When I arrived at Granada Studios on Quay Street, Manchester, the following day I was introduced to the host of the show, the legendary Bob Monkhouse. He was one of the warmest hosts I had ever met and he immediately came over to me and said 'Hello'.

The edition of *Wipeout* that I finally got to appear on also featured two female contestants. All three of us were quite nervous, but Bob put us all at ease by saying: 'Just forget about the game and the TV cameras, just imagine you're sitting in your front room and we're just playing a game on our own.' He continued: 'It doesn't matter who wins, just enjoy it, have fun, relax and don't be nervous.' He then cracked a few jokes which made us laugh and we all relaxed even further.

We then went onto the set and the production team started recording the show which took place without a studio audience present. The sound of an audience during this particular quiz show was dubbed on later.

I survived the first round but one of the female contestants was eliminated from the game. We then went into the next round and even at this point I didn't realise that this was going to be one of my most successful ever game show appearances.

I can recall that there was a round of questions on Blur song titles. I was a huge Blur fan at the time, and could even correctly guess their most obscure song titles – which the remaining female contestant didn't have a clue about! And I think this was the round that got me to the final where I had the chance to win a holiday!

Clearly I can remember Bob Monkhouse coming over to me before the final round (they used to stop the tape between rounds to check if everything was okay) and saying: 'Leon, I think you're going to do well on this subject.' I didn't know what the subject was, but, as it turned out, it was Album titles of The Beatles. By now Bob had learnt that I was a massive fan of The Beatles.

My initial thought was that I'd mess the final round up – but I was wrong! I needed six correct titles to win the jackpot prize which was a holiday. I needed my 'Wipeout Wings' to take me to Disney World in Paris, if I won.

Bob then asked me to step forward. After a few words of encouragement from him the choices of real and fake albums by The Beatles appeared on the grid in front of me and the said host started the clock. I then began making my selections on the large screen in front of me, not rushing as I wanted to make sure that I had the correct choices. Pressing the button to see how many I had got right (or wrong!), to my amazement found they were all correct! Okay, so I was a huge fan of The Beatles, but when you're in a TV studio, the camera is rolling and you're very nervous you can even forget your own name! Bob warmly congratulated me for winning and I was jumping for joy – literally!

After the recording I discovered that I had a choice of taking the holiday to Disneyland in Paris, or £500 in cash – I chose the latter! And this was on top of the £300 I had also won earlier in the show! Not surprisingly *Wipeout* became my personal favourite quiz show or game show that I have appeared on so far!

I remember cheekily asking a member of the *Wipeout* production team if I could have a souvenir *Wipeout* paperweight for my mother. She collected them and I thought this would be a lovely present for her. The team member went away to ask a higher authority if my request could be met. I was later told that I could have a paperweight for my mother – but that I'd have to pay £25 for the privilege. In the end I agreed and the cheque that I was sent after the show had the £25 charge deducted from my prize money! I'd never realised paperweights could be so expensive!

After this I successfully applied to appear on Scottish TV's hugely-popular ITV game show, *Wheel of Fortune.* This show, as you may well remember, was hosted by John Leslie and the lovely Jenny Powell. Both presenters were really friendly and I loved appearing on the show, which was recorded at Scottish TV's studios in Glasgow. Again my quest for TV fame was taking me to a place in the UK I had only read about and seen on television. Scottish TV flew me up from Luton to Glasgow and put me up in a lovely four star hotel, but Suzanne wasn't able to accompany me on this particular trip.

Prior to the recording, which took place on Wednesday 6th September 2000, we did a proper run-through in the studio and all the contestants were given a chance to spin the wheel which, was actually quite heavy! I managed to win a colour TV on the show and a *Wheel of Fortune* watch, both of which I still have, together with my *Lucky Ladders* and *Every Second Counts* watches!

Paul B: Blankety Blank *was a much-loved cheap and cheerful game show which had first been hosted by*

Terry Wogan and then subsequently by Les Dawson on BBC1. By the year 2000, ITV had decided to revive the show with Lily Savage (Paul O'Grady) as host.

Having both briefly seen O'Grady on TV just before watching a video recording of our hero's appearance on Tonight with Jonathan Ross, *this reminded Paul of his time as a standby on* Blankety Blank:

Paul W: I had successfully passed an audition for *Blankety Blank,* which was held at 2.15pm at the Jarvis Hyde Park Hotel in Bayswater, London, on Sunday 1st October 2000. Regrettably, in the event, I only ever got to be a standby on the show, and this was to be a standby contestant for the first two shows which were recorded on Friday 3rd November 2000.

Both Suzanne and Melody accompanied me to the London Studios on the South Bank, and although I didn't make it onto the show, there was a consolation prize – for all of my family! After both of the recordings Suzanne, Melody and I were taken to the Green Room to meet Paul O'Grady, Keith Duffy (from the pop band Boyzone), Michael Starke (an actor best-known for having played Sinbad in the since-ended Channel 4 soap, *Brookside*) and Julie Goodyear (best-known for playing Bet Gilroy in the ITV soap, *Coronation Street*), so that really made our day! Paul O'Grady hosting *Blankety Blank* as Lily Savage was really hilarious. Indeed, his patter off camera was even funnier (and slightly blue!) and he had the audience in absolute hysterics!

On the 13th January 2001 I went along to BBC Television Centre to audition for the snooker-based game show *Big Break*, which was hosted by comedian Jim Davidson. I was one of 800 people to audition for that particular series and I was informed that they had just 58 places available! I got onto the shortlist of 150 people but did not make it to the series.

I was then approached by the makers of the game show *King of the Castle* because it was the same team behind *It's Anybody's Guess,* and the researcher, Lauren Ebel, remembered me. Again it was made at the same South London studio which was used for *It's Anybody's Guess.* I didn't win my edition and again I walked away with a consolation prize – in this case a clock to add to my ever increasing collection of time pieces!

King of the Castle was, incidentally, quite similar in many ways to *The Weakest Link.* It was hosted by the ITN newsreader, Alistair Stewart, but the series never took off in the same way and only lasted for one run.

The next quiz show I appeared on nearly resulted in me winning life-changing money. The show in question, *Greed*, was hosted by Jerry Springer. By this point Springer had become very famous in the UK for his outrageous American discussion show which, to me, seemed to involve more attempted fights from its participants than actual conversation!

Greed was made for Channel 5 and was obviously an enthused attempt to capture the same audience and spirit as ITV1's *Who Wants to Be a Millionaire?* After applying to appear on *Greed* I was asked to attend an audition. The short-lived show had never been on TV in the UK before, so no-one really knew what it was about – myself included!

Greed was recorded on Saturday 21st March 2001 at Fountain Studios (formerly the studios of Associated Rediffusion) in Wembley Park opposite where I had worked in my Uncle Peter's shop, Preston's Food Fare, when I was younger.

Memories of working at Preston's filled my mind as I nervously entered the studios and presented myself to the production team. I certainly never imagined all those years ago that one day I would actually enter the former Associated Rediffusion Studios to appear on a programme being made there!

Basically, *Greed* involved five strangers (contestants) being put together as a team. The team had a chance of winning big money. Well, this obviously appealed to me – winning clocks and small amounts of money is fine, but life-changing money is far more exciting!

During the day that led up to the recording, and despite there being a run-through, no-one knew who was going to be on their team. As it transpired, a female contestant that I had joined for lunch during the afternoon became our team captain. The lady in question would, in time, also prove to be the cause of me leaving the studios that night without at least £10,000!

As with many shows of this nature, the TV production company recorded roughly four or five editions of the show that day. In fact, despite being called quite early on in the day, I didn't get on until about 10pm in the evening, and because of the early call that day I was quite tired by this point. One wondered whether this was done on purpose to try and prevent you from being focused enough to win great sums of money! First of all there was a round where each contestant had to answer a question. If everyone got their questions right (which we did) there was a chance for us to go on to the Big Money – hence the title, *Greed*.

We got to the £50,000 mark, so at this stage we would have won £10,000 each. However, our female team captain who, for the sake of this book I will call Tina, had the final say over whether we risked going on and potentially winning £100,000 each – or losing everything! There was also a head-to-head round (called The Terminator round) which involved attempting to eliminate one of the team members. A spotlight randomly flashed over the team. It selected one of the girls on the team, we'll call her Rachel, and she went to the front of the stage where there were two podiums positioned. She was asked by Jerry to select one of the other team members to go head-to-head with in The Terminator Round – she chose me for the showdown!

Now if you lost the head-to-head round you'd get a consolation prize of £5,000 and you were out of the game. The rest of the team could then play for the £100,000, but they would now have a £25,000 share each.

Jerry asked us to be ready with hands on the buzzers. He then asked the following question: 'Name the seaside resort featured in the sitcom *Fawlty Towers*?' Well, I was, and remain a huge *Fawlty Towers* fan so I hit the buzzer as hard and as quickly as I could and was able to answer Torquay. Jerry then said: 'Congratulations Paul, please go and stand over there while we say goodbye to Rachel who goes away with £5,000!'

Jerry then told me that I now had Rachel's share of the possible prize fund so my share was now worth £40,000 to me alone! I found myself then sitting there in a corner of the studio feeling like I was in a very surreal world! The most I had ever won to this point was £630, so this life-changing money seemed out of this world! I remember thinking: 'This can't be happening this can't be happening!'

The questions were set to get harder as we made our way up the grid to the £100,000 mark. The next guy on the team answered his question correctly, but then disaster happened and the last question was answered incorrectly. The £100,000 question was:

Which of the following films starred married couples?:

Dead Again
Eyes Wide Shut
Mr and Mrs Bridge
The Big Sleep
It Happened One Night

I chose *Eyes Wide Shut* and my team mates followed with *It Happened One Night, Mr and Mrs Bridge, The Big Sleep*. The film that we mistakenly left out was *Dead Again*, which in fact starred Kenneth Branagh and his then wife Emma Thompson. This would have won us the £100,000 of which my share would have been £40,000! *It Happened One Night* was the wrong answer, Clark Gable was not married to Claudette Colbert.

I recall that Jerry was really friendly to us all, but it was no consolation, I was left feeling so empty. I had been on the verge of winning £40,000 and now didn't have anything. In the end all I received was a souvenir photo through the post of me at the buzzer. Normally I would love souvenirs like this, but on this occasion was not a happy bunny. A photo cannot make up for losing that kind of money.

The four of us left the studios with nothing at all. If Tina had stuck on £50,000 instead of wanting to go on further, then we would have at least won £10,000 each. And that was the nearest I ever came to winning a big cash prize on a quiz show or a game show. It was a gut-wrenching moment and all of us couldn't wait to get out of the studios afterwards.

Paul B: This, however, didn't stop Paul from going further with more applications to appear on TV shows. By now he had well and truly been bitten by the TV bug again!

So where would his TV journey take him next? To my amazement I was to find out that Paul was fated to come face-to-face with the Queen of Mean, Anne Robinson, on The Weakest Link.

Chapter Nine

The Weakest Link

Having never really won anything on the National Lottery, I decided to try and improve my luck by appearing on a quiz show called *Jet Set*, which was a lottery spin-off show hosted by Eamonn Holmes.

I was selected to be a standby contestant for the show but I never got to appear on the first show I was called to attend. As I was on standby at BBC Television Centre, I was given the consolation prize of being able to select the two machines being used in that night's lottery draw! The announcer, Alan Dedicoat (The voice of the balls), said in his unmistakeable National Lottery voice: 'Tonight's lottery machine (Guienevere or Lancelot – can't remember which!) was chosen by Paul Wilder of Elstree'. Even more exciting than this I was able to meet and have my photo taken with the lovely singer Rachel Stevens. I was delighted when I later saw her do so well on *Strictly Come Dancing* in 2008.

It was then confirmed that I would be an actual contestant for the following week's edition of *Jet Set,* but the day before the broadcast I was called by a researcher from the show and told that I couldn't appear because I had recently been spotted appearing on *Wipeout*. They also knew about my appearances on *King of the Castle* and *It's Anybody's Guess*. So again I was unbelievably subject of yet another ban! This was, I thought, starting to become something of a habit!

Paul B: Undeterred, Paul successfully applied to take part in a quiz show called The People Versus.

Paul W: *The People Versus* was a great quiz show to take part in for the simple reason that it was recorded at Elstree Studios – close to where I lived! It was hosted by Kaye Adams, the one-time main presenter of ITV1's daytime show, *Loose Women*, who I remember being very friendly.

When it came for my turn on the show Kaye rattled off a host of questions and the clock slowly counted down. I started to get questions wrong and I watched my prize fund gradually dropping more and more. In the end I chose to stop at the £80 mark! There was a good crowd involved in the show and there was a great atmosphere in the Green Room at the studio both prior to and after the recording.

I next appeared in an edition of *The Biggest Game in Town* which took place at Granada TV's famous studios in Manchester on Tuesday 25th September 2001 – and it went out live! Granada paid my expenses including transport to and from Manchester and my hotel bill. However, I still laugh now when I look at a letter that the production team sent which informed me that I was only allowed a total budget of just £10 for my evening meal at the hotel the night before the recording. As if that wasn't bad enough, they wouldn't pay for any alcoholic drinks! Coming second on my edition of the show and winning the £500 cash prize, more than made up for their meanness with their hotel expenses!

I finally appeared on *The Weakest Link* after the second occasion of applying to take part on the series. People thought I was mad trying to get on the series, but I thought: 'well it's a hugely-popular series so I've just simply got to try and become a contestant!'

To get onto *The Weakest Link* I first had to take part in a short general knowledge quiz on the phone. The rule was that if you didn't get at least seven out of ten questions right, then you didn't get the chance to attend an audition. I managed to get at least seven questions right and was invited to what turned out to be the strangest audition I had ever attended.

At the auditions there were about twenty of us who were all asked to each – wait for it – pretend to be an animal! After getting over the initial shock of what we had been requested to do I wondered if I had walked into a drama class by mistake.

I chose to impersonate an orang-utan – some might say this was appropriate for me! Certainly it was all very embarrassing. I had done some embarrassing things in my time in connection with my quest for TV fame (remember my *Stars in Their Eyes* audition?) but this really took the biscuit!! I can recall we were told that we couldn't impersonate any animal that any of our fellow would-be contestants had attempted before us.

The embarrassing task of impersonating an animal also accompanied the usual task of standing up, introducing ourselves and telling the researchers etc. something about ourselves; the latter of which I was far more used to and comfortable with! Looking back on the audition now I realise it was meant to act as an icebreaker and to see how people reacted. I guess they thought if we couldn't cope with such things at the auditions, then we wouldn't be capable of facing Anne Robinson. Mind you, I always wondered how Anne Robinson would cope with such an audition. I can't see that she would have been too thrilled at the prospect of being asked to impersonate an animal such as a monkey!

On the day of recording the edition of *The Weakest Link* that I had been scheduled to take part in I made my way to the world famous Pinewood Studios in Buckinghamshire. This was my first visit to these studios and I felt as much in awe with them as I did when I made my first visit to the BBC Television Centre way-back in 1972 when I went along to take part in a recording of *Top of the Pops*.

Making our way to the actual TV studio at Pinewood, where *The Weakest Link* was recorded, my fellow contestants and I were treated to the glorious sight of the huge James Bond 007 Stage. As a life-long fan of the James Bond films this was, as you would imagine, quite a treat! There was instantly a very good camaraderie between the contestants and this helped me to relax somewhat. What I was a little disappointed with was that you aren't allowed to meet Anne Robinson before the show is recorded.

Four editions of the show were being recorded the day I was at Pinewood and I remember that I was given quite an early call time. I was amazed to discover how small the studio was when I entered and that there wasn't to be a studio audience present.

Each of the contestants were given a practice run of voting people off the show and writing on the boards – not to mention holding the boards up the right way! While this rehearsal was taking place the technicians were busy testing the lights and the music so very soon I began to feel quite nervous.

Just before the start of the recording, Anne Robinson entered dressed in her trademark black outfit for the show. She was already in character and made her way around all the contestants, including myself, and said: 'Hello'. The recording began and I got three questions wrong and was the first to be voted off! Still, I wasn't surprised and knew there was no-way I was ever going to win!

After Anne's parting words to me (which were: 'Okay Paul, who has done nothing to improve the boring image of Borehamwood, with seven votes, you are the weakest link. Goodbye.') I made my way off the set and made the huge mistake of winking at the camera. Disaster! This was not allowed as, of course, it is Anne's gimmick! The recording was stopped and the director asked me to make the walk of shame again – and not to wink at the camera! In total I had to make this walk three times until they were happy with it! This wasn't because I winked during each take, it was to make sure that the shot was right.

Then, led into a small sound booth, I was asked some questions with the aim of getting an ideal sound byte to use as I made my exit from the programme. During the five minute interview (of which only seconds were used in the actual show) they asked me how I felt about being the first to be voted off – I admitted that I was 'absolute pants!' Eventually they said there was enough footage and took me to the Green Room.

Now totally relaxed in the Green Room, I made a start on the tea and biscuits! One by one the various other contestants started to join me as they were voted off the show. I think in the end it took about two hours to record the whole show as there were stops between rounds.

I wasn't able to meet Anne Robinson after the recording as another edition of the show was being recorded straight away. However, a production assistant did manage to catch her and persuaded her to sign my copy of her autobiography: *Memoirs of an Unfit Mother*. When I was given the book back I opened the cover and on one of the first pages discovered that Anne had written the following message:

To Paul,

You were The Weakest Link. Sorry!

Love
Anne

The edition of *The Weakest Link* which I appeared in was subsequently broadcast on BBC2 on Thursday 31st January 2002 at 5.15pm. A couple of local regional newspapers ran short stories on my appearance on the show and both mentioned Anne's tongue-in-cheek reference to Borehamwood!

The quiz show *Test the Nation* was another show I took part in which was made at Fountain Studios in Wembley. I took Melody along with me, a friend, Louise, and her daughter, Natalie, but I didn't get a chance to speak. I am sure you can imagine how annoyed I was by this. Still, what chance did I have with the then future *Britain's Got Talent* judge Piers Morgan on the panel?

I had a happier experience appearing on a quiz show called *Celebrity Addicts*, which was hosted by the lovely Lisa Rogers.

Two friends helped me to make up a team for the show which was made at TVS' former studios in Maidstone,

Kent, for the UK satellite channel, Challenge. One of my friends was another game show regular, Henry Felstein, who had actually appeared on both *Strike It Lucky* and *Takeover Bid*, two shows that I had auditioned for.

My other team-mate was my friend Lorraine Silver, who had a cult Northern Soul hit called *Lost Summer Love*, when she was just 13 years old. Between us we knew so much celebrity-related trivia, yet we were still beaten during the show. The winning prize was a DVD player, which cost a lot more back in those days!

Paul B: Lorraine recalled to me her personal memories of appearing on Celebrity Addicts *with Paul:*

Lorraine: We thought we would be the dream team as our combined backgrounds in the world of showbiz covered a multitude of guises. Paul is such a character and we have become great friends. There's never a dull moment when we get together and reminisce.

Paul W: I can remember that Lisa Rogers was very pleasant and we had our photo taken with her after the show was recorded.

One day I took a phone call from a male TV researcher whose journey on the Google internet search engine had brought my name and details of my various TV appearances to his attention. He informed me that he was working on a new comedy spoof show called *GASH*, which was set to star Armando Iannucci. Iannucci was one of the writers who worked on several editions of programmes that Steve Coogan made in the guise of East Anglia radio DJ and one-time TV chat show host, Alan Partridge, and the film *In the Loop*, which starred James Gandolfini from *The Sopranos*.

The researcher asked me if I would like to take part in the show but told me – for a change – that there would be no fee. I think they were looking for someone like me in order to avoid having to pay for a professional actor! Despite this I immediately agreed to take part in the programme.

GASH was broadcast in a slot around 10pm on Channel 4. My contribution was to take the form of a one-off comedy monologue in which I played a man who had been tortured in order to persuade him to go on the game show *Wipeout*. A show, of course, that I had appeared on and no torture or amount of persuasion, as you will recall, had been required in order to enlist my services for it!

As I recorded the monologue I remember thinking that it didn't seem very funny, especially as it sent up one of my favourite hosts, Bob Monkhouse. However, the process of making the sketch was great fun.

Chapter Ten
Celebrity Spotting

Paul B: Paul and I then turned to the subject of the various celebrities that Paul has met over the years. Both of us pondered the question as to why some people become gibbering wrecks when they meet a celebrity or someone they are great fans of. Both of us admitted that it had actually happened to us in our time!

Paul W: Over the years I have enjoyed meeting celebrities of all degrees, from C-list to Z-list but on one occasion in particular I personally became a gibbering wreck!

We were out with our friends Sandie and Stephen a few weeks before Stephen's 60th Birthday in 2007. Stephen told us that they were going to have a party at their home to celebrate this very special occasion. They live in a semi-detached house in suburban Edgware, Middlesex, and they had a marquee erected at the back of the house for the occasion. Stephen is a cousin of Nicole and Natalie Appleton from the girl group All Saints, and told me that he had invited the girls to his party. He wasn't sure, however, if they would be able to attend.

On the day of the party Suzanne and I were in their front room both enjoying a glass of champagne when I spotted through the window some very well-known guests arriving at the house. I turned to Suzanne in what seemed a surreal moment and said: 'You won't believe who is walking up the drive, Liam Gallagher (lead singer with rock band Oasis), Liam Howlett (from the band Prodigy) and their partners Nicole and Natalie Appleton from All Saints.'

I have been a massive Oasis fan since their first album *Definitely Maybe* was released. I really wanted to talk to Liam Gallagher but at the same time I wanted to be cool, and especially as we were at a private party, not an Oasis fan club meeting!

The All Saints girls seemed very friendly and were chatting to people at the party. I asked Sandie if she would introduce me to Liam Gallagher. Sandie agreed and took me over to Liam and said: 'Liam I'd like you to meet my very good friend Paul.' Liam shook my hand and said in his strong Manchester accent: 'Hello mate, how yer doin'?'

For some inexplicable reason I suddenly lost the ability to speak! After saying: 'Hello Liam it's nice to meet you,' I couldn't think of anything else to say, so I think I said: 'So Liam, are you going to do any more solo stuff?'

He replied: 'I don't do solo stuff, everything I do is for the band.'

I felt really stupid. I'm meant to sound like a well-informed fan but instead came out with that stupid question! The rest of the conversation with Liam was a 'Blur' (ironic really as both the bands Blur and Oasis are arch rivals!). I was very happy that I managed to get my photo taken with him just before he left the party.

Paul B: On Saturday 7th October 2000, the England national football team lost to our old foes Germany 0–1 at Wembley, That night, however, Paul booked a small restaurant in London's West End to celebrate Suzanne's birthday:

Paul W: We went to a fish restaurant called Sheekeys. Now I am not a great fish eater but I was able to get a nice and expensive battered cod and chips there. It was a special occasion and we went with our friends Simone and John. Also in the restaurant was one of the England footballers that had played in the disappointing match that afternoon – none other than David Beckham together with his wife Victoria (Posh Spice). The four of us were very excited to be in the same restaurant as the Beckham's. I actually had a quiet word with the maitre'd and asked if it was possible to get autographs for my daughter Melody, he replied: 'No Sir, we don't allow that here.' I was disappointed but expected that would be the answer.

At one point during the evening Suzanne and Simone went to the Ladies downstairs. As they came out of the Ladies David Beckham came out of the Gents. He smiled at them and they were both frozen to the spot! This would have been an ideal opportunity to ask for an autograph and I am sure he would have obliged but they were both speechless. When they came back to our table they were like two gibbering schoolgirls! They might not have come back with an autograph, but they did at least now have the memory of being as close as they were ever likely to get to the legend that is David Beckham!

Paul B: I then asked Paul if either he or the members of his family had spotted any celebrities whilst abroad:

Paul W: Since Melody was one year old we have spent many a holiday on the Costa del Sol. Like millions of Brits, the short flight and the almost guaranteed sunshine is the main attraction.

Puerto Banus is a small port with numerous boats, some of them extremely large. The front line of Puerto Banus is an array of designer boutiques and restaurants. It also attracts the rich and famous. In fact I can clearly remember Melody coming back one night and saying that she had spotted Cilla Black in the port.

On another occasion we were with friends Simone and John and had left our respective offspring in the safe hands of a baby sitter for the evening. On the way back to the apartment we stopped at a pub called the Robin Hood. On this particular evening they were having a Karaoke night, which was being hosted by a member of the famous 1960's group, Dave Dee, Dozy, Beaky, Mick and Tich. I think it was 'Tich' hosting, but it could have been Beaky.

Another famous celebrity was in the pub – the one and only Lionel Blair. He was called to the stage and, as ever, didn't need to be asked twice. He gave a rousing version of *New York, New York*.

We rented an apartment close to Puerto Banus for several holidays. One year Des O'Connor was also renting an apartment there. I said 'Hello' to him one day and reminded him that we had met at a Water Rats ball several years earlier. I also told him that one of my closest friends David Phillips, who I had appeared on several game shows with, was once a contestant on the revived quiz show *Take Your Pick* that Des hosted. I asked Des if he remembered the said occasions and when he said 'No'. I resisted the opportunity to say 'Dong' to his reply! Joking aside, Des seemed a very pleasant and polite man.

Paul B: Knowing that Spain was a favourite holiday destination of the Wilder family, I asked what other memories they have of their various trips there:

Paul W: We have had some of our best holidays in Spain – but we have also had, to date, the worst-ever holiday there as well.

It all started when we missed our flight to Malaga. It was a Bank Holiday weekend and we arrived late for our early morning flight by just fifteen minutes. The plane had actually not taken off, but as we see regularly in various airport-related TV documentaries, there was no way they would let us through the check-in desk.

After a period of begging the answer was still an emphatic 'No!' The only flight that I could get us on to was from Bournemouth Airport. This wasn't ideal as at the time we were at Luton Airport.

The saving grace was that one other family had arrived at the check-in desk at the same time as us. So I organised the Bournemouth flight with this other family and we made our way on the train to Christchurch Station in Dorset. We eventually got to Bournemouth Airport only to be told that our flight was to be delayed for three hours! We did eventually get to Malaga, but some fourteen hours after we were due to arrive.

This particular holiday went from bad to worse. I got bitten on the eyebrow by a mosquito, and my eye swelled up as if I had been in the ring with Lennox Lewis. I saw the doctor and he swiftly gave me a jab in the lower part of my back. This was possibly the worst holiday that I have ever had and I am now always extra early for the airport.

Returning to celebs, I have spotted publicist Max Clifford on several occasions. We were in a café called Madhatters, which was featured in a series called *Marbella Belles*. It's a great location for a fry-up if Suzanne wants to look around the market at the Bullring. Max Clifford was on the next table enjoying his brunch.

Other sightings have included: former GMTV presenter Fiona Phillips, football commentator Andy Gray, and even Malaga's number one son, Antonio Banderas. You can also quite often spot an array of *Hollyoaks'* stars and various reality TV stars – but you can't have everything. Sorry, just joking!

Paul B: Meanwhile back to the main plot. Paul then took part in a recording of the BBC1 daytime show, Stars Reunited. *This was hosted by Dale* 'Supermarket Sweep' *Winton at the Riverside Studios in Hammersmith, London.*

Paul W: The edition of the show that I took part in was a real wander down memory lane for me as it featured *Top of the Pops.* Thoughts of my appearance in the crowd during one of the shows back in 1972 came flooding back as I watched the guests on the show – Tony Blackburn, Dave Lee Travis, Alan 'Fluff' Freeman and the legend that is, and will always be, Jimmy Saville – being interviewed.

I was given the opportunity to ask a question to Jimmy Saville during the show, although it was a pre-prepared question. The question was: 'Jimmy, how did you get all your famous catchphrases?' This then gave Jimmy an excuse to launch into an entertaining monologue about how his much-loved catchphrases had come about over the years.

I was to find myself in the company of one Dale Winton again when I appeared on a game show that he presented called *I'm The Answer*. This short-lived series was broadcast on ITV1 during the week at around 5.30pm.

When I arrived for the show, accompanied by my friend Richard Bunt, there were about 150 people in the audience. Everybody present was asked to answer a question posed by Dale Winton by writing on a board. They were then required to hold the board up. Those who got the answer wrong were eliminated and this continued until there was enough contestants for the show.

To my amazement I correctly answered a question on cheeses. The question was: 'Name a blue veined cheese?', to which I held up my (*I'm The Answer* board) with the answer – 'Stilton' – now written on it. I was surprised that my cheesy answer was correct, as I really hate cheese! In fact I could have been a contender for the TV show *Freaky Eaters* as I am quite a plain fussy eater! Anyway, I was one of the four people present to qualify and be asked back to appear as a contestant on the show the following day. I didn't do very well when it came to the actual show and subsequently went away without a prize. Still it was great fun appearing on it.

Paul B: Reaching your fiftieth birthday is quite a milestone and Paul's turned out to coincide with a very eventful few days. At this point in the proceedings I touched on the subject and this inspired Paul to recall the events connected with the period around his half century:

Paul W: Having thrown a party the week before, we were now about to embark on a special birthday surprise holiday.

My mate Wayne is a day younger than myself so we quite often celebrate birthdays together. As this was a 'big one' our wives Suzanne and Elayne had saved up to treat us to a really special trip!

We were booked to fly out to our destination of Las Vegas on Wednesday 2nd March 2005. The night before our journey we popped over to see my parents. We returned home to finish our packing when I received a phone call from my brother Martin to say that he was over at mum and dad's and that he thought that dad had suffered a stroke. We dropped everything and went back over there to find dad lying on the floor. His face was contorted and he was unable to speak. An ambulance was called and not surprisingly we were all frantic with worry.

The ambulance duly arrived after what seemed like an age. By this time my dad's paralysed condition had started to ease. He was taken to Barnet General Hospital where we were informed that it appeared as if he had had a 'mini stroke'. The hospital ran some tests and dad began to feel a lot better. They kept him in for the night and I decided to stay there with him. Our flight to Las Vegas was due to go the next morning and I had to make a decision as to whether or not to go ahead with the trip.

By 4:00am my dad was sitting up in bed and telling me that I must go ahead with the holiday. I spoke to the medical staff, they confirmed that it was a mini stroke and he seemed to be over the worst.

I left Barnet General at about 4:30am and went to see if my mum was ok. She had one of her three-times-a-week dialysis treatments coming up that morning. She also insisted that the show must go on and I should go on the planned holiday.

The decision was made and after no sleep that night we made our way to Heathrow Airport with our friends Elayne and Wayne. I kept in touch with my dad's progress by text with my brother.

When we arrived at McCarran International Airport in Las Vegas, Suzanne and Elayne had arranged for a white stretch limo to meet us and take us to the Mirage Hotel on the famous strip. By this point I was mega-tired from the exhausting trip and the worrying events of the night before but we were determined to crack on with the celebratory trip. We indulged ourselves with an enormous salt beef sandwich from New York's famous Carnegie deli, which has a restaurant within the Mirage Hotel. I followed this with a giant slab of chocolate fudge cake and ice cream.

That first night in Vegas we even took a cab to the downtown area of Fremont Street to check out the bright flashing lights and penny slots. We eventually crawled into our king size beds and went straight to sleep.

The next morning feeling far more refreshed we decided to chill out by the pool. All of a sudden I heard familiar voices. Our friends Simone and John together with Karen and Joe had all arrived to spring a birthday surprise on me. I was delighted and totally amazed that our friends were joining us and had made the trip all the way out to Vegas!

After a relaxing day we went to eat at the Top of the World Restaurant at the Stratosphere Tower. The food wasn't the best we had ever tasted but we did have sensational panoramic views of Las Vegas as the restaurant is located some 800 ft above Vegas and revolves 360 degrees every one hour and twenty minutes.

On Friday 4th March 2005 we took the Helicopter tour to the bottom of Grand Canyon. Only Karen (Smiffy) opted out of this as she had taken a similar tour some years earlier. For Suzanne and I it was our first trip in a helicopter. So the seven of us nervously boarded the Maverick helicopter. We were fitted with noise reduction headsets and voice activated microphones allowing us to communicate with the pilot and each other.

Once we were airborne the nervousness subsided and the helicopter seemed to glide along at a nice and easy pace. The views were sensational as we flew over the Hoover Dam before landing at the bottom of Grand Canyon by the Colorado River. We got out of the helicopter and had some champagne and snacks before the flight back to Las Vegas. This was not a cheap excursion, but certainly one I will never forget!

On our return to the strip we strolled through the shopping mall at Caesars Palace and the Forum Shops under a ceiling that is painted to replicate a beautiful blue sky. Las Vegas is certainly an adult's playground where everything is over the top and larger than life – very me! Not everyone's cup of tea, but I loved it! That evening we went to Mystere, one of the *Cirque du Soleil* shows, at the Treasure Island Hotel. I have to admit I was so tired that I fell asleep during the show.

I was born on a Saturday and here I was some fifty years later waking up on Saturday 5th March 2005 a long way from Kingsbury NW9. I was in Las Vegas, Nevada. After a relaxing day, a big night was planned that would run into Wayne's birthday on Sunday 6th March 2005.

We started the night at a theatrical show called *Tony 'n' Tina's Wedding*. This show was at the Rio Hotel but has since moved to the Planet Hollywood Hotel. The idea of the show is that the audience members actually play the roles of Tony 'n' Tina's family and/or friends and the main principal's at the wedding are of course actors. It is a very funny and entertaining show. It is apparently one of the longest running off-Broadway shows in history.

Following Tony 'n' Tina's Wedding, we were offered complimentary tickets for another show in another part of the Rio Hotel. The Rio Hotel is appropriately named, as there is a carnival atmosphere in the hotel. As we collected our tickets in the hotel for our next show, colourful fantasy floats glided above us to the background of lively Latin music. The show we saw was a real treat for us guys. It was called *Eroktica* and basically featured sexy, topless cabaret dancers, choreographed to classic rock hits. It was obviously a tough show to watch, but someone had to watch it! We ended a great night by going up to the VooDoo Lounge at the top of the Rio Hotel for a nightcap.

All in all it was a great trip to celebrate my big one with some of my close friends in the bright lights of Las Vegas. As I previously said, 'it's not everyone's cup of tea, but I loved it.'

I am delighted to say that my dad made a complete recovery from his 'mini stroke' and it was great to see him fit and well on my return.

Paul B: By this stage Paul was starting to appear less and less on TV in quiz shows and game shows. In fact in 2005 he didn't appear on any at all. This was the year that Suzanne began to work part-time as a film and TV extra.

Paul W: Suzanne and I had a couple of very good friends who have worked as extras (or background artists) for several years and whenever we saw them Suzanne would always say: 'Oh I'd really like to do that.' Tony Zitren, who has been an Elvis Presley impersonator for many years, steered her in the right direction for bonafide extras agencies to register with. A tip for budding extras: never pay an up-front joining fee. Most reputable agencies will deduct their annual fee from the first job that they get you.

Melody had now reached the age of 18 and had started working full-time thus granting Suzanne some more spare time. With that she decided the time was right to try and seek out some work as a film and TV extra. So through Tony's recommendation Suzanne registered with the right agencies and to my amazement one of the first jobs she was offered was on the BBC soap, *EastEnders*. Suzanne began by appearing in scenes as someone who attended Ian Beale's engagement party in the Queen Vic.

I started to feel very jealous and I decided there and then that I should try and get involved in this kind of TV work.

Paul B: Paul didn't realise it at that point, but he was set to tread an even more enjoyable and rewarding path as part of his quest for TV fame.

Chapter Eleven
Extra Time

By now the family jewellery business was being broken up and I knew I was set to have a little more time on my hands. As a result I thought that some part-time work as a film & TV extra would prove to be ideal for more than one reason. Don't get me wrong, I had enjoyed appearing regularly on the game shows and quiz shows, but they didn't always prove very profitable! Working as a film & TV extra, however, would at least, I thought, also lend me the opportunity to receive some kind of an appearance fee as well as the thrill of working, if only in a small way, on a film or a TV production of some kind.

With this decision formed in my mind both Suzanne and I started making ourselves available to agencies for film & TV extra work. We also made it clear to the various agencies that we signed to that we were a couple. This, as it turned out, proved to be a good idea as we now tend to be offered jobs as a couple six or seven times out of every ten. So not only do we now get to work together, but it also saves petrol if you are both travelling to the same studio or location.

Paul: I then asked Suzanne her thoughts on working as a film & TV extra both with and without Paul:

Suzanne: I very often get jobs as an extra with Paul. We are often cast as a couple, which works out quite well because we sometimes have to be at locations at five in the morning and this could be in the middle of nowhere! Paul usually wakes me up with a cup of coffee and then drives us to the location but, sadly, this is the nearest I have ever got to the superstar treatment.

I remember that on one occasion Paul was very envious of a job I was booked on without him. It was working on Harry Potter and the Order of the Phoenix. *It was an early call time on a very rainy Sunday morning. The location was Westminster Underground station where the extras were required to play commuters (Muggles) going up and down the escalators while Daniel Radcliffe was passing us. To Paul's credit he drove me there early in the morning and even came back to pick me up at the end of the 'shoot'.*

Paul W: When my first job finally came through I was over the moon – it was to work as an extra for a day on the ITV1 police series, *The Bill*. Suzanne and I were both given the chance to work together on this booking on Friday 6th October 2006, and we made the nightmare journey down to TalkbackThames' studios in Merton Park. This is the studio complex where the company also used to record the soap *Family Affairs*, for Channel 5. Both Suzanne and I have been huge fans of *The Bill* for many years, so to actually find ourselves at the studios was, of course, very exciting.

Paul B: The Bill, *as all hardcore fans will know, was first made and broadcast by Thames TV on 16th August 1983 as a pilot episode (entitled* Woodentop*), and became a mainstay, regular series on ITV from 16th October 1984.*

The Bill is set in and around a fictitious police station in Sun Hill, a fictional borough of Canley in East London.

Paul W: After signing in and being briefed on what they wanted us to do, Suzanne and I were driven to a nearby location which turned out to be a hotel. Here we were required to play hotel guests sharing a drink or two together in the bar.

Graham Cole (PC Tony Stamp) appeared in the scene we were asked to appear in. It was a very enjoyable part and everyone was very welcoming and friendly. In fact everybody that I speak to who works in the industry as a film & TV extra says how much they enjoy working on *The Bill* as there is such a great atmosphere down at the studios.

An added bonus is that there is a very good canteen! This was an aspect of the production which the former *Birds of a Feather* actress Pauline Quirke also commented on in an interview that I read recently!

To our amazement, and probably due to the speed and professionalism of the cast and crew on this particular unit of *The Bill,* we found ourselves being cleared to go at lunchtime.

My second role as an extra was working on the BBC1 soap, *EastEnders*. I was very excited but very disappointed when I discovered that my scenes were not to be in the Queen Vic or on the Albert Square lot set at BBC Elstree. No, I was called to play the part of a mourner at a funeral which was being shot in a cemetery opposite a hospital in Watford. This was the same hospital where Melody had been born some nineteen years previously!

At first I wondered whether the funeral scenes being shot were for a major character that was being killed off in the series, but I was wrong. The funeral turned out to be for a short-lived character called Evie Brown (Marji Campi), the ex-wife of a character called Bert Atkinson. Both the actor playing Bert Atkinson (Dave Hill) and Pat Evans (Pam St Clement) were present at the day-long 'shoot'. As with *The Bill* the *EastEnders'* extras were a good crowd and I really enjoyed the camaraderie.

Paul B: Paul informed me that by now he was starting to become acquainted with the lingo required when you work as an extra. He then explained some of the more amusing terms one needs to know as an extra when you are on set:

Paul W:
Best Boy: This is not a description for the most popular male on the set, but is apparently a term for the first assistant electrician who assists the Gaffer (the head electrician).

Dolly: This is a term for the equipment which carries the camera on tracking shots.

Gel: Not something used when one gets sore on set, but is a term for something which covers a light to create different lighting effects.

Honey Wagon: This term amuses me the most as this is the technical term for the toilet when on set.

Redhead: Not a description for one of the female crew members, but a term for a type of light.

Squib: This is apparently an explosive charge used to create the effect of a bullet or a small explosion.

On Tuesday 31st October 2006 I found myself working in another enjoyable role, that as an extra working on the film *The Bourne Ultimatum*.

Paul B: The Bourne Ultimatum *was a spy film sequel to* The Bourne Supremacy *and starred Matt Damon as Jason Bourne.*

Paul W: All of the extras – and there were many of them for this 'shoot' – were based at a pub in Waterloo Station in London, and the scenes we were called for were being shot in Waterloo Station itself.

The extras, including myself, present were just required to walk through the station and play commuters or people waiting to meet friends or relations.

During the filming of one scene I can vividly recall that the actor Matt Damon, who was being chased, brushing directly past me. I am not sure if this shot made it into the final cut because I must admit I have never seen the actual completed film.

I must also confess that the first time I saw Matt Damon at the location I didn't recognise him, although I was more than aware of who he was. I do recall, however, that he came across as a really friendly guy.

Whilst I was working as an extra on *The Bourne Ultimatum* I got speaking to some of my fellow extras there that day. The discussion, as it always is amongst extras, was about productions you'd worked on that year and what work you had coming up. Well, very soon the conversation turned to a new film that was soon to be made called *Run Fatboy Run*. This was a film that was set to feature the former *Spaced* sitcom co-star, Simon Pegg.

The gossip was that the film required extras to play marathon runners in certain scenes in the production. I asked which agency was arranging the extras for the marathon scenes and it turned out that the agency in question was one that I had signed up to but so far I had not received any work from them.

After I was cleared from working on scenes for the day on *The Bourne Ultimatum* I started to make my way home. During the journey I called the agency that were looking for marathon runners and told them that I was willing to play one of the runners in the film.

So having been offered extra work on *Run Fatboy Run,* I found myself at a location near to Tower Bridge in London, very early in the morning on Sunday 12th November 2006, standing in the cold dressed as a marathon runner. While I tried to keep warm I began speaking to one of the other extras present at the 'shoot'. Before long I realised that I was standing next to the director on the film, who turned out to be David Schwimmer (Ross Geller in the American sitcom, *Friends*), who was making his directorial debut on the film.

Eventually the filming got underway and I was included in scenes where the various marathon runners in the film are seen warming up for the fictitious race. Friends have since told me that they have spotted me in the released film as I appeared standing behind some of the main characters in one of the scenes.

Following my work on *Run Fatboy Run* I found myself working as an extra again on an episode of *The Bill* on Friday 15th December 2006. Suzanne and I again worked together on this booking and needless to say it was a really enjoyable 'shoot'.

Chapter Twelve
Big Brother's Ever-Willing Big Mouth

I have always watched and been a great fan of *Big Brother* since the show started during summer 2000. I became a huge fan of the *Big Brother* spin off show *Efourum* and its sequel *Big Brother's Big Mouth*, both hosted by the comedian Russell Brand.

Since 2002, *Big Brother* has been filmed at Elstree Studios in Borehamwood, Hertfordshire, a short drive from our home in Elstree. The *Big Brother* spin-off shows are also filmed near to the *Big Brother* house at Elstree Studios.

One evening I was watching *Big Brother's Big Mouth* and wondering just how one went about becoming a member of the audience on the show, when I spotted someone I knew, a DJ called Ian Leigh, in the studio. I was intrigued when he was asked for his comment on a *Big Brother*-related subject during the actual programme. I thought: 'I want to be on this show.' Not least because I am not shy on TV or afraid to offer my opinion – especially on *Big Brother*-related matters!

A few days later I happened to see Ian at a function where he was working as a DJ. I took him aside during his break and asked how he had managed to get onto *Big Brother's Big Mouth.* He said he had a friend in radio who had taken him along and so he didn't know how you exactly went about obtaining tickets.

A few months later and prior to the start of *Celebrity Big Brother 2007* I saw an advert on a website called 'Be On Screen' which said that the makers of *Big Brother's Big Mouth* were looking for 'loud and lively people' to take part in the new series. Both Suzanne and I agreed that I fitted the description so I wrote a letter and rather than send it I left it for the programme's researchers at security at Elstree Studios.

Shortly I received a call from a researcher called Amy Fernando on *Big Brother's Big Mouth* who said they were interested in my joining the audience for a pre-series edition of the show which would not be broadcast. It would be a sort of a warm-up show to give Russell Brand and the production team a practice run-through.

The researcher asked me all kinds of *Big Brother*-related questions in order to assess whether I really was a fan or not. My knowledge of the programme was deemed suitable and extensive enough and I was subsequently given a date and time to attend the rehearsal programme. I was told that if they liked my contribution during this production then I would be invited to join the audience of a broadcast edition of the show during the upcoming series.

It must have been instinctive but when I arrived in the *Big Brother's Big Mouth* studio I grabbed a seat dead centre in the front row. When the rehearsals got underway Russell Brand, complete with his Kenny Everett-esque microphone came over to me and asked me which celebrities I would like to see in the *Big Brother* house during the new series of *Celebrity Big Brother.* I replied with a line which to this day I believe got me onto the show, which was: 'You want to get that b***h Naomi Campbell in the house and see how she gets on!'

Okay, it wasn't subtle but it did the trick, and the line went down very well with the audience and apparently the researchers, as I became a regular on the show from then on. I think they realised that I wasn't afraid to talk and say what I thought!

During my first edition of *Big Brother's Big Mouth* I managed to get a chance to speak and thus offer my humble opinion both sides of the break. In fact it soon became to be a bit of joke amongst the other regular members of the audience that I got to know on the show that they knew I wanted to say something at least once either side of the break!

Incidentally, Phil Cornwall and former *Catchphrase* host Roy Walker were just two of the guests of *Big Brother's Big Mouth* on the four editions I appeared on during *Celebrity Big Brother 2007.*

A memorable event that happened during one of the four shows I appeared on during that series was that

Russell Brand decided to come and present a greater part of the show while sitting on my knee. This he did while he also had his arm round me. I wasn't too sure about him sitting on my lap, but of course the camera would be focused on us so I was more than happy to put up with him bouncing on my knee! Following this show I managed to get a great photo taken of Brand with me. Other photos of me taken during my visits to the show during that series included one with singer Leo Sayer the day after he famously broke out of the *Big Brother* house!

I was thrilled when I was invited along to the final edition of *Big Brother's Big Mouth* for that series. I think they invited me because I had been one of the more forthright speakers on that run of the show.

Prior to the broadcast I was taken along with the other guests and invited audience members on the show up to the Green Room where we were offered food (things on sticks) and a glass or two of champagne. Here, I spoke to several of the guests appearing on that edition of the show: Vanessa Feltz, Amanda Lamb, Rustie Lee and Paul Morley. As Paul Morley and I are both huge music fans I was thrilled to be able to chat to him and share our mutual passion for the subject.

Incidentally, I recall that during one of my first *Celebrity Big Brother's Big Mouth* shows the audience was not boisterous enough in the first half of the show. As soon as we went to a commercial break, Russell Brand took off the top of a bottle of water and shouted at the audience: 'Come on you f*****g b******s – liven up!,' and threw the water over the audience! I was sitting at the end of the front row so the water missed me but it did spill over the studio floor! The floor manager and the crew had a frantic few couple of minutes mopping up the water before we went back on air.

My thoughts on Russell after watching him host four live shows and a pilot were that he was an absolute lunatic but incredibly funny at the same time. He's not everyone's cup of tea but an off-the-wall comedian who could go on to bigger and better things – and he has certainly done that!

On Tuesday 9th January 2007, Suzanne and I were booked to appear as extras on a scene in the TV series, *Cape Wrath*. The location for *Cape Wrath* was situated somewhere in Kent, and it turned out to be a pretty dull job as we spent most of the day sitting in an extras bus in a supermarket car park! There were just three of us present in the bus, Suzanne, myself and another extra, and I think we waited for about six hours in total before we were called to the set. It wouldn't have been so bad if we could have gone onto the set to look at the filming, as I enjoy watching the crew setting up the camera, the lights etc. Instead, a member of the production team kept popping their head into the bus and telling us to continue waiting while they filmed other scenes.

At about 6pm, now all feeling quite bored and tired, a member of the team came and called us to the set which was a mocked-up building made to look like a hotel. There was a car positioned outside the building and our job was to look out of the windows of the mocked-up hotel and to act surprised as the car was blown up! With this one scene finished we were allowed to make the hour-and-a-half car journey home.

My next role as an extra was playing a solicitor on another edition (episode 517 for the record!) of *The Bill* on Sunday 11th March 2007. I had to escort a prisoner through the foyer at Sun Hill police station. Again this was great fun and it was good to be back working on the series again, if only for a day.

On Friday 20th April 2007, Suzanne received a call from one of the extras agencies we were signed up with to ask if we would be available the following Monday. Suzanne replied that we could be. She was then asked if we both had valid passports, which we had. Suzanne was becoming more and more intrigued as the call went on! They wanted us to work for a small production company who were making an advert for Transmanche Ferries which would be shown in the ITV1 Meridian area. We were told that it would be a day 'shoot' and we would be filming in Dieppe in France. It sounded great and we looked forward to the filming the following Monday.

On the Monday we drove down to a farmhouse in Kent where we were met by an independent producer and his cameraman. They then drove us to the Channel Tunnel and we were taken across to France.

On arriving in France we were driven to the port of Dieppe where we were filmed looking at the various local tourist attractions, including a church and a boulangerie, as if we were a tourist couple making a day trip to France. The last part of the filming took place on a Transmanche Ferry and this transported us back to England. All in all it was a good day out, although very tiring!

A tip for all new budding extras is that you should always get signed out at the end of a days 'shoot' and obtain a copy of the 'chit'. Being slightly naive and with the producer telling us that he doesn't do chits because the agency knows him well, we did not insist on a signed chit. It turned out to be the longest time that we ever waited for a payment – around four months to be exact – and we fell out with the extras agency in the process. Also, the promised DVD of the advert failed to arrive so we never did see it!

The next extras work I was given saw me working on a film called *Miss Pettigrew Lives for a Day*. This was a period drama set in the 1920s. I was called to a costume fitting (which you get more money for attending) a few days before the 'shoot' and was fitted out for a 1920s suit, hat and shoes. I was also given a 1920's haircut, which I wasn't too happy with, as I like to have my hair quite long.

Paul B: Miss Pettigrew Lives for a Day *is a romantic comedy directed by Bharat Nalluri. The cast of the film includes: Frances McDormand and Amy Adams.*

Paul W: Working on the film was very enjoyable. I remember that we were based at The Strand Palace Hotel in London. Filming took place early on a Sunday morning and everything was made to look like it was the 1920s in the immediate area around The Savoy Hotel.

My role (and that of the other extras present) in the scenes filmed that day was to cross the road while two main cast members were being filmed having a conversation. As the morning went on tourists started to congregate around the location to watch and asked to have photos taken with the extras in their period costumes. This, of course, made it impossible for the filming to continue and they wrapped up the day at about 11am.

Both Suzanne and I then played parents to two children in the pilot of a new game show called *Holiday Fever*. This programme which I don't think ever made it to a series was on location at Stansted Airport and was not broadcast. I recall that both Jeremy Edwards and Sarah Cawood were presenters on this pilot although we only ever saw Jeremy Edwards.

The summer of 2007 heralded the arrival of *Big Brother 8*, and I thoroughly enjoyed appearing on a total of fourteen editions of *Big Brother's Big Mouth* during that series! By now Russell Brand had decided to leave the series and a host of celebrity guest presenters were being drafted in to host a week each on the show. The first edition I appeared on in that series was hosted by the politician George Galloway, possibly best known for his appearance as a purring cat with Rula Lenska on

Celebrity Big Brother in January 2006. Other guest presenters that series included Pete Burns, who I am no great fan of either. Fortunately the attractive presenter Amanda Lamb (who I do like!) was also one of the guest speakers on an edition I appeared on during that series, so that more than made up for having to appear with the aforementioned guys.

The day after housemate Emily Parr was removed from the *Big Brother* house for using an offensive word, a member of the *Big Mouth* production team called me and asked if I would appear on the show that Friday. I said 'yes', but admitted I was surprised, as back in those days they didn't like to have the same people appearing more than once in a week. The researcher informed me that they wanted to have known sensible people on that particular show who wouldn't make any stupid remarks about the word that Emily Parr had said to her fellow housemate, Charley Uchea.

The researchers on *Big Mouth* that series were virtually letting me pick which dates I wanted to appear on the show, so I was spoilt for choice! Friday nights – eviction nights – were certainly the best nights to be at Elstree Studios to appear on *Big Brother's Big Mouth* as the atmosphere was so great and you were invited along to spend time in the marquee which the studios had put up for the show. This acted as a Green Room on eviction nights.

On one edition of *Big Mouth* I thought the former Visage singer Steve Strange was going to engage in a fight with me! The show that week was being presented by the very attractive actress and TV presenter, Thaila Zucchi.

By tradition I tend to say things on the show that seem to go against the grain and on this occasion I decided that I would make some positive comments about housemate Charley Uchea, who was proving not to be too popular either inside or outside the *Big Brother* house. In fact my very words were: 'Charley has the figure of *Baywatch*, the face of *Crimewatch* but she is going to be one of the biggest stars of this series!' With that, Strange, who was by this stage perspiring profusely, his eyes out on stalks, looked at me and shouted: 'You need your f*****g eyes testing, you are talking s**t!' I just laughed. By now poor Thaila was trying to calm the situation in the studio.

Looking back, I wish I hadn't taken that remark from Steve and simply laughed. I would have liked to have made a comment back, but at the time I was just so taken aback! I still think it was one of the weirdest *Big Mouth's* that I have appeared on – I am sure Thaila thinks so as well!

During the series a researcher on *Big Mouth* asked if I would attend one of the rehearsal programmes that were held on Monday nights at the studios. These were organised in order to give the chance for the guest presenter/s that week to get used to how the show worked. I, of course, agreed and found on my arrival that it was to be a certain Peaches Geldof who was presenting the show that week. I had never met her before and I must admit that I found her to be very sweet. For one so young and inexperienced at TV presenting she did quite well. She spoke to me several times during the run-through and although perhaps she was a bit nervous with the technical side of things, Peaches certainly had an air of confidence beyond her 18 years.

On the actual Friday night live show I sat at my usual front row end seat and had my regular *Big Mouth* mates: Chris 'Mini Mario' Parry and Marlon 'Diet on the Dance Floor' Williams, alongside me. Needless to say there was never a shortage of things to say with us on the show and I think this made things easier for the young Peaches.

For me, the other memorable guest presenters during that series included Mathew Horne and James Corden (from the BBC3 sitcom *Gavin & Stacey*). They were excellent during their week on the show and I really enjoyed being in the audience while they were presenting. I think their success on the show is probably the main reason why they were asked to present *Big Brother's Big Mouth* on E4 during *Celebrity Hijack* in January 2008.

As Mat and James realised I was one of the regulars that they could have a joke with, they decided that every time one of them came over to ask my opinion they would poke me on the chin with the famous long stick microphone. They jokily apologised as I continued to air my views. They were the best presenters of *Big Mouth* since the days of Brand and I was not surprised to see that they have gone on to become household names.

Being a great Arsenal fan I was thrilled when the former footballer and Gunners legend, Ian Wright, hosted a week on *Big Mouth,* and was even more thrilled when he asked for my opinion during the show. After the show was finished I quickly approached Wrighty for a photo. Moments later he was mobbed by the *Big Mouth* audience. Nowadays, the audience for *Big Mouth* are not allowed to take cameras or mobile phones into the studio. In fact, they search you, and your mobile phone is taken off you before entering the studio. The threat of immediate eviction from the studio if you are found with a mobile is made clear to everyone.

I was lucky enough to be invited to the finale edition of the *Big Brother's Big Mouth* during that summer and I had the chance to meet most of the housemates. I even managed to have my photo taken with Samanda (AKA twin housemates Sam and Amanda).

Paul B: Professional photographer, and good friend of the hero of our story, Scott Kleinhesselink, contacted me to offer his thoughts on Paul and their first meeting on the Big Brother's Big Mouth *set:*

Scott: My partner and I first met Paul on the set of Big Brother's Big Mouth *during the Brian Belo era on* Big Brother. *It was our first time on the show and I distinctly remember a very distinguished and eloquent gentleman (Paul Wilder) providing a very good bit of data for the show. I was really impressed with how much he knew about* Big Brother.

As the shows continued and we were invited back it always seemed to coincide with Paul's participation on the show. I would make it a point of talking to him and as time went on we all became regulars on the show. Of course Paul was more well-established than us.

The conversations we had with Paul were always enjoyable as we discussed the show and tried to predict who was going to be evicted and who would win. Paul always had it right!

We even worked together on some screen test shows for BBBM *and it seemed as if the celebrities testing out for* BBBM *had an immense respect for Paul. It was almost as if they were hoping for his approval and a positive reaction from him in order to ensure their selection for the show.*

Blenda and I continue to enjoy working with, and knowing, Mr Wilder!

Paul W: Also during the summer of 2007 (on Wednesday 4th July to be exact) I gained further extras work on an episode of *The Bill*. This time I played a reporter at a press conference. So far I had been, on the whole, very lucky with the extras work I was being offered – and things were just about to get even better!

After drinking the cappuccino that left me feeling 'spaced out'.
Left to right: Elayne Myers, yours truly, John Hooper, Suzanne,
Graham Rabin, Simone Hooper, Yvonne Rabin.
The equally 'spaced out' Wayne Myers somehow took this smiley photo.

Just before taking off for an amazing flight over the Grand Canyon
in March 2005. Left to right: Simone Hooper, Elayne Myers, Suzanne,
Joe 'Joey Boy' Reiselson, yours truly, Wayne Myers, John Hooper
and the 'Maverick' Helicopter pilot.

With Russell Brand after my very first appearance
on *Celebrity Big Brother's Big Mouth*.

Thumbs Up! With singer Leo Sayer the day after he broke out
of the *Celebrity Big Brother* house in January 2007.

I was so excited to meet Arsenal legend Ian 'Wrighty' Wright when he hosted *Big Mouth* for a week in 2007.

With Bollywood star Shilpa Shetty in the *Celebrity Big Brother's Big Mouth* studio. This was shortly after the actress won *Celebrity Big Brother* in January 2007.

With the very attractive actress and presenter Thaila Zucchi after my run-in with Steve Strange on *BBBM*.

Meeting Dermot O'Leary at the *Big Brother Celebrity Hijack* Final in January 2008. This was O'Leary's last ever *Big Brother* appearance.

Presenting for Israel's Channel 2 Keshet TV during the filming of a *Big Brother* documentary at Elstree Studios in 2008.

That really is David 'The Hoff' Hasselhoff – not a waxwork! Taking a break from the filming of a sketch for *The Sunday Night Project* in July 2008.

It was great to meet the quirky and eccentric David Gest,
a one-time *I'm a Celebrity Get Me Out of Here!* contestant.

Host of *I'm a Celeb ... Now!,* Mark Durden-Smith,
who inspired me to go ahead with this book.

My first *London Marathon* in 2003 dressed in one of Elton John's jump suits!

Dressed as Sgt Pepper for the rainy *2004 London Marathon*.

Yeah Baby! I'm dressed here as Austin Powers for the *2005 London Marathon*.

After a four year gap I ran my fastest marathon in 2009 at 4 hours 39 minutes and 17 seconds.

After 5.5 miles in the *2009 London Marathon*, I overtook Katie Price (Jordan) and Peter Andre just two weeks before they split up.

Suzanne was more than happy to meet celebrity chef Jean-Christophe Novelli in May 2009.

Paul Wilder looks on as Jean-Christophe Novelli writes a good luck message on the manuscript for this book in May 2009.

A publicity photo of Paul Wilder from 2007.

Here I am with the two gorgeous ladies in my life:
my daughter Melody and my wife of 23 years, Suzanne.

Chapter Thirteen
Checking Into Hotel Babylon

Suzanne and I decided to join yet another extras' agency during 2007. Whilst we were attending an interview at the agency's London office we were asked if we would both be free the forthcoming Thursday to work as extras on an episode of the BBC1 drama, *Hotel Babylon*. Do cats like milk? Do ducks like water? As *Hotel Babylon* was one of our favourite programmes we jumped at the chance!

The following Thursday we made our way to *Hotel Babylon's* warehouse location in Aston Clinton in Buckinghamshire. As with the cast and production team on *The Bill*, we found everybody on *Hotel Babylon* to be really friendly and supportive. The hotel's exterior set was built inside the warehouse building together with the hotel's reception, bar, restaurant, lift and bedroom sets.

Both Suzanne and I played hotel guests in this particular episode and could be seen pretending to share a conversation with Max Beesley's character, Charlie Edwards, in the foyer. Because we were featured in this way we had the bonus of receiving extra (if you pardon the pun!) money.

Max Beesley was really pleasant, he shook our hands and we had a great chat in the lobby of *Hotel Babylon* before we filmed our scenes near to the reception desk.

Looking back at my notes for that year I realised that prior to working on *Hotel Babylon* on Saturday 28th July 2008 I also worked as an extra on the film remake of *Brideshead Revisited*, another period piece.

I was required to attend another costume fitting before my filming call date. This was fine but I wasn't too pleased to find that I would be required to have my hair cut again. Still for this indignity I also received an extra addition to my fee – £28! Despite this I no longer will accept bookings to do costume dramas if I am required to have my hair cut! The scenes, incidentally, which I took part in for *Brideshead Revisited* were filmed at Agnews Art Gallery on Old Bond Street in London.

During August 2007 I was booked as an extra to appear in a film called *National Treasure: Book of Secrets*. Once again a costuming fitting was required – although no haircut was called for this time. I played a priest in the film – what a job for a good Jewish boy! In fact, as I recall, there were ironically at least ten Jewish men playing priests there that day! The scenes I took part in were filmed on the steps of St Paul's Cathedral in London, and were part of a car chase sequence.

On Saturday 29th September 2007 both Suzanne and I played passer by's in scenes filmed in a park in central London for the popular BBC1 drama, *Ashes to Ashes*.

Although we didn't get to talk to the series stars, Philip Glenister and Keeley Hawes, we did take part in scenes which they were involved in.

Holby Blue was a short-lived police spin-off series to the medical dramas *Holby City* and *Casualty*. Suzanne and I both took part in a day shoot as extras on this series. We were told to meet the unit at a location just off of Deptford High Street in South East London.

There were several extras called for on this shoot and we were all squashed into two very crowded extras busses and taken to an office block location in Deptford to play party-goers at a cocktail party. Suzanne was originally cast as a Superintendent but when they saw she was only 5'1" and she was totally lost in the uniform they replaced her with a 5'8" supporting artist.

It was a long day's 'shoot', finishing around midnight. But a bonus came in the form of the presence of the lovely *Footballers Wives'* actress, Zoe Lucker.

Paul B: Having taken part in scenes as an extra on Holby Blue, *Paul was delighted when he received a call from one of the agencies he was signed up to and asked to play a patient on* Holby City. *As with* EastEnders, Holby City *is recorded at BBC Elstree just down the road from where Paul lives.*

Paul W: On the first day that I was called I took part in a scene as a patient which was taped at 9.10am. I could be spotted in the final scene wandering through one of the wards at the hospital which in actual fact is the Neptune Building at BBC Elstree. This building was also famously used as a location in the since ended long-running children's drama series, *Grange Hill*. I then sat and waited in the Green Room until 6.10pm but wasn't called during the rest of the day.

I was, however, called back the following day but wasn't used for any part of it! So I experienced yet another long wait in the Green Room! But, of course, I was paid and waiting around goes with the territory of being a film & TV extra – you learn to accept it. During one of my days on *Holby City* I was delighted to be able to share a little chat with one of the series' stars, Robert Powell.

It was then back to working on *The Bill* again for Suzanne and I for two more episodes. During the filming we were lucky enough to get the chance to chat to former *EastEnders'* star Louisa Lytton who was at the time playing PC Beth Green in *The Bill*.

We were filming scenes set in a shopping centre (Suzanne and I played shoppers) and, deciding not to bother with the standard issue catering truck, Louisa Lytton popped over to a fast food takeaway during the lunch break and came over and sat with the extras. She was lovely and I know all of us were really touched that she came over and spent time with us.

Catering is usually pretty good on 'shoots' and it's always appreciated when stars queue with the extras for lunch. They could have their meals taken to the trailers or they could even pull rank and jump the queue of supporting artists. Suzanne told me that the star of *The Sopranos*, James Gandolfini, joined the queue for lunch the day that she worked on the film *In the Loop*.

Paul B: Paul then recalled to me that in October 2007, he celebrated Suzanne's 'special' birthday by throwing a party for their friends at Bushey Golf Club; and a special weekend away that was to follow:

Paul W: Suzanne and I love a good party and this was great fun even if I say so myself!

We had live music which was provided by John Ellis, a brilliant Elton John tribute act. I also arranged for our very good friend Tony Zitren, an Elvis Presley impersonator, to perform a few songs towards the end of the evening. So we celebrated Suzanne's birthday in style! What Suzanne didn't know was that I had secretly arranged to take her away on a European break the following weekend with some of our closest friends.

I wanted us to visit a city that we had not been to before but that was not too far away. After discussing it in total secrecy with our friends, Amsterdam was deemed the most suitable of destinations.

I did tell Suzanne that I was taking her for a surprise weekend away. But all I said was 'bring your passport' and I suggested what clothes to take as I had checked the weather forecast for Amsterdam.

On Friday 12th October 2007 I woke Suzanne with a coffee in good time before our 'taxi' picked us up. When the 'taxi' arrived, it was actually our good friends Elayne and Wayne who were driving us to Luton Airport where we were boarding an Easyjet flight to Schiphol Airport in Amsterdam.

After playing the guessing game during the journey to Luton Airport, Suzanne finally realised that we were bound for Amsterdam after seeing the flight times on the information board. We checked into the NH Grand Hotel Krasnapolsky in Dam Square. The hotel is well located in the centre of Amsterdam close to the house of Anne Frank, the Red-Light District, the Van Gogh Museum and not forgetting the Heineken Brewery.

The weather was good, we had a bit of lunch and then went to visit Anne Frank's house. Elayne had pre-booked tickets to avoid the long queues to get inside the legendary house. It was incredibly interesting. Anne Frank and her family hid in the house for two years from the Nazis during the occupation of the Netherlands. The 13-year-old Anne Frank wrote her widely-read diary there, which chronicled her life from the 12th June 1942 to 1st August 1944. It has been translated into many languages and has become the basis for several plays and films.

After the visit to the house we strolled across the bridges of Amsterdam and took a canal boat tour. This was both relaxing and interesting. Following our boat trip we went for a coffee in a 'Brown Café'. I have never been into drugs in any shape or form. I might have had the odd puff of a joint when I was younger, but I have never been a smoker of even cigarettes, this simply did not interest me. I have always preferred to have a few drinks in order to unwind.

We chose to go to a coffee shop called Abraxas, which was down a side alley, a block from Dam Square. It had three floors and had the mixed aroma of coffee and weed wafting through it. The four of us sat down and perused the menu. A selection of regular drinks was available together with hash cakes and hash milkshakes. Suzanne and Elayne decided to have a regular coffee and a hash muffin each. Wayne and I went for a cappuccino each. For an extra three euros you could have a 'spaced out' cappuccino, so we opted for that.

I must have appeared like a real virgin tourist as far as ordering those coffees went as the very friendly girl behind the bar explained to me that I should keep stirring my cappuccino as I drank it. It was a small cup and the contents tasted quite bitter, so I added sugar and kept stirring as instructed. Suzanne and Elayne were nibbling at their muffins and seemed quite calm and relaxed, as did Wayne.

When we left the coffee shop I was feeling quite heady. By the time we had walked the couple of blocks back to our hotel my head was starting to feel like it was spinning. Back up in our room, Suzanne asked if I had any chest pains, which I didn't. So she just thought I was a silly old 'stoned' fool and hoped that I would eventually sleep it off as we had arranged to meet Elayne and Wayne at 8pm for dinner in the adjoining room.

Wayne had fallen asleep for a couple of hours and was pleasantly stoned. I was still quite hyper but couldn't get off the bed. I didn't know what day of the week it was, although I was aware of what was happening I had no control over it. I tried to get off the bed once again but I couldn't stand up and fell back giggling. Suzanne sighed and resigned herself to room service.

At around 11pm there was a knock on our hotel room door. Another surprise, I had arranged for Suzanne that four of our close friends – Simone and John and Yvonne and Graham – would join us that evening. Having heard of the days events, they came to see how I was.

I have no idea how they did it, but they somehow managed to get me down to the hotel bar. I spent the next few hours laughing hysterically at the slightest thing. I pointed at my friends individually, and for no apparent reason I would burst into uncontrollable fits of giggling. My facial muscles had relaxed and I was gurning for England! Suzanne apologised to our friends for my behaviour but they recall that they had never laughed so much.

The following morning, most of whatever was in that cappuccino had worn off but as we strolled along the sunny streets of Amsterdam I must confess that I felt a slight paranoia. I was sure people were looking at me even though they probably weren't. After lunch I was feeling a lot better and we took in further tourist attractions. Tram rides led us to the flower market which is apparently the only floating flower market in the world. It was a wonderful, colourful place to see.

We then stopped off at the famous Sex Museum, which was hilarious. It was really interesting to view the photographic history of pornography through the ages. The seven foot long phallus-shaped vibrating chairs certainly gave the ladies a smile!

The phrase 'When in Rome' sprang to mind as we visited a live sex show in Amsterdam's Red-Light District. Almost all these sights were within walking distance of our hotel. We soon found a place called Casa Rosso. We queued and paid 30 euros for the 'pleasure'. After watching the choreographed 'acts' for about half an hour, it all became a bit boring so we left. The weekend of sex, drugs and rock & roll in Amsterdam was certainly eventful!

I have been told that the drug in my coffee might have been called Laughing Buddah, but I can honestly say that despite the hours of laughing I would not want to repeat the experience. In future I will stick to a couple of Voddy's or a couple of glasses of Rosé to get me merry.

After a great holiday, and finally returning to the UK on Thursday 15th November 2007, I made my very first appearance on the spin-off show of ITV1's *I'm a Celebrity Get Me Out of Here*. The spin-off discussion show, broadcast on ITV2, was entitled *I'm a Celebrity Get Me Out of Here … Now!*

On the first edition I appeared on as one of the audience contributors, *Coronation Street's* Becky Granger (Katherine Kelly) was one of the guests. Through sheer determination I managed to get to speak during the show and I really enjoyed being part of the production. A later edition of the show found me sitting next to former children's TV presenter Toby Anstis. In a live link up to Australia, Toby, myself and a couple of girls posed questions to Rodney Marsh, John Burton-Race and Kate Hopkins, who were fresh from leaving the jungle!

I appeared on one show a week during that series of *Get Me Out of Here … Now!,* and on my third edition Vanessa Feltz was a guest on the show. I was really pleased when Vanessa recognised me from appearing as one of the audience contributors on *Big Brother's Big Mouth* and we had a lovely little chat.

Paul B: Andy Cooper, one of Paul's fellow audience members and friends from I'm a Celebrity Get Me Out of Here … Now!, *kindly recalled to me:*

Andy: I will always remember how the researchers on the programme used to shuffle the show regulars around so it didn't look like the same people were on all of the shows! 'You can't sit on the front because you were on the front row last time,' was a regular cry that used to come up from the researchers. But their efforts were always thwarted when the great unwashed got to the front row and immediately contracted 'startled bunny syndrome' the moment Mark Durden-Smith asked them a question on camera! He would then be desperately looking around for anyone he knew who would actually be able to speak on live TV and always ended up with Paul Wilder. Sometimes he was known to practically jump over people in the audience to get to him on the back row! Watching the camera crew trying to follow him was often the highlight of the evening. TV is always at its best when it goes wrong, and on I'm a Celebrity Get Me Out of Here ... Now! *things went wrong a lot!*

Chapter Fourteen
A Return To Walford

At 8.30am on Wednesday 5th December 2007 my phone rang. The voice on the other end of the line said: 'Paul, can you get to BBC Elstree for 9am to appear as an extra on *EastEnders*?'

Talk about short notice! This is another aspect that goes with the territory of being a film & TV extra. 'No problem,' I said. The caller was from one of the extras agencies I am signed up to. I instantly re-arranged my day to get to Clarendon Road for 9am.

By 9am I was in the *EastEnders* reception area at BBC Elstree. Even at the time I was signing in I had no idea what they wanted me to take on for the day or how long I would be there for. I was directed to go and wait in the extras' Green Room (a portakabin!) which, on arrival, I discovered to be empty! It was just me. I was informed that they would call me when I was required.

Eventually with no call materialising I decided to wander back to the reception area as I was feeling quite lonely! I started to make conversation with the receptionist and then glanced out of the window, but by now it was raining heavily.

A short time later some of the main cast members from *EastEnders* began to make their way through the reception area. Eventually I spotted the lovely actress Samantha Janus, who plays the role of Ronnie Mitchell in the series, entering the reception area. Janus, who you may think originally came to fame in the BBC sitcom *Game On*, actually represented the United Kingdom in the *Eurovision Song Contest* in 1991 where she came tenth with the song *A Message To Your Heart*. The song eventually reached No. 30 in the UK singles chart.

Samantha smiled and I decided to do the very British thing of trying to strike up a conversation by mentioning the weather as an opening. It worked and this started a short conversation. It's always reassuring when the people you admire on television turn out to be so pleasant when you meet or even work with them.

From the reception area I then went into the canteen where, as I sipped on a cup of tea, I spotted Steve McFadden (Phil Mitchell) sitting in the corner of the room. However, I thought it best to leave Steve to his coffee and paper.

Eventually I was told that I would be playing a photographer and I was sent to wardrobe where they fitted me for a different jacket to the one I was wearing. To my amazement I discovered that the scene I was to appear in would be at the end of one of the episodes. This is what's technically known in the trade as a 'duff duff' moment, so called because it's the final 'cliff-hanger' scene of the episode that closes with the famous opening to the *EastEnders* theme tune: Duff … duff … etc.

The scene in question featured Minty (Cliff Parisi), Heather Trott (Cheryl Fergison) and the actress Lisa Ellis, playing a newspaper reporter called Marni. My role was as a well-behaved and non-speaking photographer carrying a selection of heavy photographic equipment.

In the scene we arrived at Minty's flat and discovered that we couldn't take Minty's wedding photos there as he had smashed the flat up! The reporter then suggested that we take the photos at another location. As I had no dialogue to speak I didn't know how to react. So in a split second, having not been told how to react, I decided to ad-lib a nod! Because so many people that I know saw me in this duff duff scene I have become famous for my nod! My nodding expertise has since been put to good use in the opening episode of *Reggie Perrin* – but more of that later.

I really enjoyed working on *EastEnders* and hope I will be asked back again one day. I know that my wife Suzanne enjoyed her brief time working on the soap as well.

After this I worked as an extra for a day on a TV drama series which was originally called *The Last Van Helsing*, but later was changed and went out under the name of *Demons*.

The scenes I was required to take part in as an extra were filmed at the Royal Festival Hall in London. All fifty or so extras there that day (including myself) were required to be filmed sitting together in a block in the auditorium. We were then moved several times to sit together in a block in various parts of the auditorium.

During post production the shots were pieced together to make it appear as if the auditorium was totally full! What a clever way of saving money. It wasn't possible to see that it was the same people in the shot, even though we weren't required to change clothes, because we were filmed at a distance from the stage.

Soon I got a call to work as an extra on yet another episode of *The Bill*. This time I played a mourner at the funeral of PC Emma Keane (a character played by Melanie Gutteridge). Then it was back to BBC Elstree for another day on *Holby City* where I played a member of the hospital board.

We filmed in a room in the Neptune Building at the studios which was made to look like a board room. When the episode was broadcast you could quite clearly see me in the scene sitting at the large table wearing a bright yellow shirt!

A flower garden in a park in an area of Paddington in London was to be the location of the next TV extra work that I did with Suzanne. This was for the popular sitcom *After You've Gone*, which starred Nicholas Lyndhurst and Celia Imrie.

I had met Nicholas Lyndhurst at a Water Rats charity event twenty years previously. Although I did get a chance to meet Nicholas during the filming, I didn't mention that I had previously met him as I was certain he wouldn't have remembered the experience!

I recall that David Jason was also present at the Water Rats event and that both he and Nicholas Lyndhurst sat on the top table and they were mobbed for their autographs! This was during the height of *Only Fools and Horses*' popularity and it seemed like everyone in the room wanted to have their photo taken with them – including me, of course! They were really patient considering both actors are quite shy, unlike their characters. In the event, I managed with sheer dogged determination to obtain a photo with the two actors and it remains one of the favourites in my collection.

Meanwhile, back to *After You've Gone*. The filming location both Suzanne and I were called for were for scenes at a wedding. The filming was really enjoyable and we finished by 1pm, which was a bonus as we still received a full days pay!

The next extras work I was offered was for an ITV drama called *Mr Eleven*. This included the *Doctor Who* actress Michelle Ryan in the cast. She was delightful and I found myself sharing a cup of tea and a Cherry Bakewell over the tea trolley during a break from the filming.

Another delightful actress I have been lucky enough to come into contact with whilst I have been working as an extra is Connie Fisher. TV fans will remember that Connie came to fame when she won the Saturday night BBC1 show *How Do You Solve a Problem Like Maria?* Now, having wowed both critics and public alike in the role of Maria in the stage version of the musical *The Sound of Music*, Connie was appearing as Gemma Atkins, an Elvis Presley-obsessed traffic warden, in an ITV1 drama series called *Caught in a Trap*.

Both Suzanne and I were lucky enough to be asked to appear as extras on *Caught in a Trap,* and we found ourselves at an auction room location in Surrey where, not surprisingly, auction room scenes were being filmed for the one-off drama which was to be broadcast over Christmas 2008. When the programme went out you could only see a shot of my back, but you could clearly see Suzanne bidding in one of the auction room scenes. Unfortunately, I forgot to record the drama and Suzanne has, understandably, never forgiven me!

Another great TV job that both Suzanne and I worked on as extras was ITV2's *Secret Diary of a Call Girl*, which stars former *Doctor Who* side-kick, Billie Piper.

We had two days filming on the drama and the scenes we took part in were filmed near Chorleywood in a small village called Sarratt. There were only a few extras present but they were a really great crowd and over the two days we all became quite close. The first day we filmed scenes for a christening in the village church and on the second day we took part in scenes set at the post-christening party. To this day, given the subject of the drama, I still laugh at the fact that the pub we filmed the party scenes in was really called The Cock Inn!

Later, while I was working as an extra on an Ikea advert, I got a call from a researcher who worked for an Israeli TV company. She told me that they had been given my telephone number by the makers of *Big Brother's Big Mouth*. She then went on to explain that Israeli TV Channel 2, Keshet TV, had just purchased the rights to *Big Brother*, and prior to making the first series of their own version of the show they were making a documentary about the UK version of the series. They were planning to send over a documentary film crew to film footage of the first night of *Big Brother 9* at Elstree Studios.

Then came the main reason for the researchers call, she asked whether I would be interested in attending the filming and help explain everything to the crew and assist in presenting the odd section for the documentary. I told her that I was very interested and asked how much my fee would be. There was silence and then, after regaining her composure, she laughed and replied: 'We're Israeli's, Mr Wilder, we don't pay.' Quick as a flash I replied: 'I'm Jewish, and I want to be paid!' Unbelievably they did agree to pay me a fee. So after all these years of trying to gain some paid TV presenting work I had finally realised my dream!

On the opening night of *Big Brother* on Thursday 5th June 2008 the Israeli TV crew picked me up from my Elstree home and drove us the short distance to

Elstree Studios in Borehamwood. The security was very tight at the studios for the launch night of *BB9*.

The start of filming was of me interviewing members of the crowd including two girls who were queuing at the side of the studios. They were waiting to enter the studios' site and gathered near to the *Big Brother* house to watch the new housemates enter the compound.

The crew then took me into the studios and Davina McCall in her pre-show warm-up kindly mentioned that there was an Israeli TV company present to film a documentary that night and she asked the crowd to give them a big cheer, which I thought was a thoughtful welcoming touch. Davina shouted: 'Shalom' to the Israeli film crew. I was placed by the side of the stage so that I could be filmed watching the proceedings.

The crew from Keshet TV asked if they could come to my house the following night (Friday) and film me with my family watching *BB9* on Channel 4.

It just so happened that we had invited our friends Yvonne and Graham with their twins Jodie and Jeremy around for dinner that night. I asked them if they minded that a TV crew would be joining us to film us watching *Big Brother*. They didn't mind – in fact they were quite excited at the prospect!

After the excitement of filming at the *Big Brother* house on launch night, things were now becoming even more surreal as we were still eating our Friday night meal when the crew arrived! Forget *At Home with the Osbournes*, this was *At Home with the Wilders!* It was hilarious as the crew interviewed Suzanne, Melody and our friends.

After hours of filming over the two days the amount of footage used in the final cut of the documentary was not a great deal but I was very happy with the DVD that was presented to me. This included footage of me interviewing some of the crowd, some zoom-in shots by the stage and of me explaining the phenomenon that is *Big Brother. At Home with the Wilders* was not included! I really enjoyed the whole experience and was very pleased with how welcome they made me feel.

My next TV extra work was on another Channel 4 TV show. This time it was as part of a sketch on *The Friday Night Project*. This has since moved to Sundays and become known as, wait for it, *The Sunday Night Project*, and is co-hosted by the two brilliant comedians Justin Lee Collins and Alan Carr.

I noticed on *StarNow* website that the production team of *The Friday Night Project* required extras to appear in a sketch which would feature David Hasselhoff. The Hoff was to be co-presenting an edition of *The Friday Night Project* and one of the inserts in the show would see him taking part in a Jeremy Beadle-style 'hit' on a member of the public. This was set to be filmed at a location in Hackney in the East End of London.

On turning up I was disappointed to find that my face would not be seen on TV as all of the extras were required to wear masks with The Hoff's face on it! The sketch was to see all of the extras playing members of a cult dedicated to The Hoff.

After the successful completion of the 'hit' on the member of the public who had been set up by a friend, I was able to get my photo taken with The Hoff. David turned out to be very professional and had time for everyone, behaving like a real star should. It was a great pleasure for me to meet him that day.

Another job that I found through the *StarNow* website was for the *JML Shopping Channel*. Most jobs on these types of websites usually pay below the going rate and sometimes don't pay at all. However, I saw an advert with words to the effect of: 'Earn £100 for talking about pop music'. I thought, 'That sounds good to me', so I applied. I received a call from the guy producing the advert and he told me it was for a new classical boxed set of CDs. I said: 'Hang on a minute, I thought the advert was for pop music?' The guy replied: 'Well, I put pop music because I didn't think I'd get many replies if I put that it was for classical music.' I replied 'But I don't know anything about classical music!' The guy told me not to worry, as he would send me a box of classical CD's to listen to. 'You'll recognise a lot of them from TV adverts,' he said, 'You'll be able to blag it!'

The CD's arrived and after playing about a minute of each of them I did indeed recognise many tracks. I accepted the assignment and went up to a tiny studio in Kentish Town. I was filmed as a talking head giving a testimonial about the pieces of music on the CD's. When I was asked about my favourite track, I simply said *'Nessun Dorma'* as it was used as the theme song for BBC television's coverage of the 1990 *FIFA World Cup* in Italy. The job took about 10 minutes in total and turned out to be an easy £100!

Chapter Fifteen
The Quest Continues

It was back to Sun Hill police station again for Suzanne and I. Well, actually this time the scenes we took part in for *The Bill* were filmed at the Park Plaza Hotel in the West End of London.

In between takes, we were told to go and relax in the lobby of the hotel while the principal actors – Simon Rouse (DCI Jack Meadows), Chris Simmons (DC Micky Webb) and Cat Simmons (DC Kezia Walker) continued without the extras.

It was during a break from the filming that a Canadian woman came up to Suzanne, me and another extra and asked us for our autographs. She said she had been watching us filming in the lobby of the hotel and on the stairs that led to the first floor. As far as the Canadian lady was concerned we were actors in *The Bill* and she wanted our autographs. We happily signed.

I made just five appearances on *Big Brother's Big Mouth* during the summer of 2008. In fact it was July before I was allowed to make my first appearance in the audience on that series. I was a bit disappointed but realised that I had been spoilt the previous year. Despite this, appearing on the show was great fun as usual.

Caroline Flack, Bianca Gascoigne and Keith Lemon (Leigh Francis) were just three of the presenters on the show who were given a week respectively to host in the series. I really enjoyed appearing when they were presenting the show and managed to give my opinions on the housemates to each of them on screen.

I also managed to appear on an edition of *Big Brother's Big Mouth* during the last week of *Big Brother 9* when the lovely Davina McCall was having her turn at hosting the show. She was excellent and I think this is one of the reasons why she is now set to be the permanent host of *Big Brother's Big Mouth,* as well as the eviction night shows. Meeting Davina on *Big Mouth* that night completed meeting the trio, for me, of *Big Brother* presenters: Russell Brand and Dermot O'Leary being the other two. I met Dermot in the *Big Brother's Big Mouth* studio on the final night of *Big Brother – Celebrity Hijack*, during January 2008.

The summer of 2008 saw me writing a *Big Brother*-related blog for the *Borehamwood & Elstree Times*. This gave me another outlet to vent my spleen on the housemates that year.

It was now time to book into *Hotel Babylon* again with Suzanne for more extras work. By now former *EastEnders'* actor Nigel Harmon had taken over from Max Beesley in playing the manager of the hotel.

Actor Christopher Cazanove was playing a hotel guest who suffered a heart attack in this particular episode that we worked on as extras. Oh, and the veteran actress Janet Brown (who is the widow of the *Carry On* actor Peter Butterworth) was also on set and was very pleasant to speak to.

I was disappointed in only being able to make just five appearances on *Big Mouth* during the summer 2008, but the eight appearances I made on *I'm a Celebrity Get Me Out of Here ... Now!* during November 2008 more than made up for it!

During that year guests on *I'm a Celebrity Get Me Out of Here ... Now!* included David Gest who came fourth on *I'm a Celeb* in 2006. In my opinion Gest should have won that year but lost out to Matt Willis who won with Myleene Klass and Jason Donovan coming second and third respectively. However, by appearing on the show he turned around the public's perception of him and he came across as a very funny and quirky personality.

David received a rousing reception from the *I'm a Celeb* crowd and when interviewed by host Mark Durden-Smith he proceeded to mention as always his cleaner Vaginika Seaman. I was thrilled to have a chat with David after the show and have my photo taken with him.

As a fan of the original version of the BBC sitcom *The Fall and Rise of Reginald Perrin*, which starred the much-missed actor Leonard Rossiter, I was excited to be given the opportunity to appear as an extra on the new re-make of the series, *Reggie Perrin*.

In the new version of the series the role of Reggie Perrin is played by former *Men Behaving Badly* actor, Martin Clunes, and it was he who I found myself speaking to during a break from filming. The scenes the extras had been called up to appear in on this particular day were being filmed on a train which travelled to and from Princes Risborough and High Wycombe all day whilst the various scenes were shot.

I mentioned earlier that I used the good old fashioned British subject of the weather as a successful ploy to start a conversation with the lovely actress Samantha Janus. Well, I decided this would be a good way of striking up a conversation with Martin Clunes. It worked again! Finding myself lucky enough to be sitting practically opposite Martin in the train carriage it made it easy to hold a conversation with him. He seemed a genuinely nice guy.

Law & Order UK was another great production to work as an extra on. I think I appear playing a solicitor in episode eight of the series. I was given the opportunity to spend two days working on *Law & Order UK*, which was filmed in a warehouse at a location in Surrey.

On set I found myself sitting next to a female extra. My seat could have come straight out of an episode of the original version of *The Fall and Rise of Reginald Perrin* as it had this embarrassing habit of making noises like a fart each time you moved around on it! This fact will be important later!

Seated directly in front of me and my female extra colleague was the very sweet *Doctor Who* actress, Freema Agyeman, actor Ben Daniels and former *Minder* actor, Patrick Malahide. As we were working on set for most of the day we, the extras, got to nodding or smiling terms with the main actors and actresses in the series. Now, during a break from filming I happened to move around on my chair and in doing so the chair made one hell of a farting noise! Freema instantly turned around laughing and thinking that the sound in question had been emitted not from the chair – but me! Ever one for playing the fool, instead of explaining what had caused the noise, I found myself pointing at the female extra sitting next to me and saying: 'It was her!' Freema still laughing said: 'That's hysterical, not that you made a farting noise, but that you blamed it on her.'

Law & Order UK seemed a really happy set and I was very pleased to return in January 2009 to play a jury member.

At the time of writing the most-recent TV extra work that I have had was a day on the new BBC remake of *The Day of the Triffids*. This filming took place in Rainham in Essex. It was a very, very cold and late 'shoot' in which all of the extras including myself had to pretend we had been blinded by the Triffids!

Yes, my life as a film & TV extra has certainly been varied and far from ever being dull!

Paul B: Our conversation then turned to the London Marathon. Paul recalled how he used to watch the London Marathon *on TV and dreamt about taking part. I then asked him what led him to fulfil this dream:*

Paul W: In 1983 I seriously thought about training for the marathon and even managed a 10 mile training run. However, back in those days I was young, free and single and I was still partying and drinking. I must admit that having fun seemed a far easier (and more enjoyable) option than training! For twenty years I watched the *London Marathon* and still had the dream of taking part in what is, to this day, still a phenomenal event.

For Christmas 2001 my lovely wife Suzanne decided to buy me a running machine. Was she trying to tell me that I was putting on weight? This annoying machine became an incredible dust collector as I rarely used it. But after Suzanne moaned so much to me about what a waste of money it was I decided to start using it – if only for the sake of a quiet life! Of course, being the type of person who never goes over the top with things, within a few weeks of using the running machine I decided that I would apply to take part in the *London Marathon*.

The process in applying for a place to run the 26.2 miles involves a ballot. Approximately 35,000 runners take part but there can be around 100,000 people actually applying to run. A total of 20,000 'public' places are allocated through the ballot. However, if you do not get one of these places you can request a *'Golden Bond'* place through one of the many charities.

I didn't get a place through the ballot so I ran for the charity *Diabetes UK*. My mum has been diabetic for many years and my dad had been recently diagnosed for Diabetes.

When you sign up for one of the *Golden Bond* charity places you are obligated to raise a figure of around £1,500 for the charity in question. I am pleased to say that I raised nearer the £3,000 mark. After securing my place in the marathon the hard work of training for it was next on the agenda.

In November 2002 I downloaded from the internet an eighteen-week 'novice' training schedule, which consisted of training runs 4 days a week running distances ranging from 4 miles on Tuesday, 9 miles on Wednesday, 5 miles on Thursday and the very important 'long run' at the weekend. The long runs build up to 15, 16, 18 and 20 miles, as you get closer to the actual marathon day. The 20 mile run is three weeks before the big day – you never run the 26.2 miles in training. I was told it's similar to the way racehorses are trained. If a horse is running, say, a 2 mile race, it won't run 2 miles in training but will be trained to reach its peak for race day.

After completing the 20 mile training run you then taper down the mileage putting the energy back in your body, ready to peak on the big day. It can be likened to a boxer not wanting to leave a fight in the gym.

During my months of training I learnt a lot of other lessons about: Joggers nipple, Runners trots and chafing in the nether regions. I logged on to some runners forums and learnt the answers to some literally very painful problems!

Joggers nipple: This is caused by the friction of rubbing against your t-shirt. It can be so bad they bleed. The prevention is to apply *Vaseline* to your nipples and cover with a large plaster before you start your training run.

Runners trots: These are caused by the motion of running and this loosens you up in more ways than one! I was once in quite a bit of distress 9 miles from home with not even a pub or field in sight. The prevention is to try and have a 'clear out' before you start a long run and then take a couple of *Imodium Instants*. This should help.

Chafing in the Nether Regions: This is caused by the friction of your running shorts and can be very painful. Prevention is back to that very important pot of Vaseline. Spread generously.

I started my training schedule and thought about the amazing fancy dress runners that add colour to the *London Marathon* every year. Surely I wasn't thinking of attempting my first marathon with the additional handicap of a costume? What do you think?

In December 2002, Elton John opened a shop for his 'Out of the Closet IV' sale in London's Regent Street, where he was to sell off hundreds of his costumes to raise money for his Aids Foundation.

I'm a big Elton fan so I went along to have a look. Elton wasn't there himself, of course, but I did see Lulu browsing in the shop. She looked great as ever. Funnily enough, Lulu performed at the fiftieth birthday party of one of my friends in 2008. She was sensational and brought the house down with one of my favourite songs, *To Sir With Love*. Anyway, amongst some amazing costumes out of my price bracket I found an electric blue soft leather jump suit made by Gianni Versace in 1973. I bought it for £75 and donned it for the 2003 *London Marathon*.

Sunday 13th April 2003 finally arrived and with all the training over, today was set to be 'The Big Day' and a day in which I was to achieve an ambition that I first decided upon some twenty years previously.

I made the way to the start at Greenwich Park wearing my Elton John's jump suit and *Diabetes UK* vest, I started my jog. The atmosphere was unbelievable. Everyone was chatting, the camaraderie with other runners was brilliant and the pavements of London were lined with around 500,000 people cheering on all the various runners. My fancy dress paled into insignificance as I was overtaken by Wombles, Elvis Presley's and the odd Rhino. Those Rhino costumes looked like they weighed a ton! However, 4 hours 58 minutes and 32 seconds later I crossed the famous finishing line after passing Buckingham Palace in The Mall. My runner's number, incidentally, was 43732.

As the medal was placed around my neck, a feeling of elation took over from the true feeling of exhaustion. I had achieved another personal dream – and it was partly thanks to Suzanne inspiring me by buying me that bloomin' running machine!

Suzanne, Melody and some of our friends met me and after I went to the *Diabetes UK* meeting point for a well earned massage (a perk of taking part in the race!) we travelled home by train where anyone with a London Marathon Medal was treated like a hero! Complete strangers on the train were congratulating all the marathon runners. What a day! Having achieved this ambition I had the crazy idea of doing it all again! What a glutton for punishment I am!

In 2004 – dressed in a yellow Sergeant Pepper's costume – I again competed in the *London Marathon* (this time for the charity *PHAB Kids*) and the weather was decidedly on the wet-side. The rain, however, didn't dampen my spirits and on this occasion I finished in 4 hours 43 minutes and 15 seconds. Incidentally, 32,101 competitors started the marathon that year and 31,679 finished.

The year 2005 heralded the 25th Anniversary of the *London Marathon* and I think Paula Radcliffe ran in this race. My finishing time that year was 5 Hours 25 minutes and 29 seconds. This time I ran in a full Austin Powers costume complete with wig and frills – Yeah Baby! I ran in aid of the *National Kidney Research Fund* as my Mum had now been on kidney dialysis treatment at Watford Hospital three times a week for over five years. Probably due to the weather being too hot, I passed out soon after completing the marathon that year, but recovered after a few minutes.

The week leading up to the *London Marathon* in 2009 was quite exciting. With most of the training completed, I was left with some simple short runs to keep me loosened up: 3 miles on Tuesday, 2 miles on Wednesday and 2 miles on the Saturday.

On Monday 20th April I received a call from one of the extras agencies I am signed to. They had put me forward for a *Marks and Spencer* advertisement, which would be filming that Wednesday. On Tuesday I was in a meeting with my accountant when the agency phoned with apologies – I did not get the *Marks and Spencer* advert. However, they could put me on a 'shoot' for the BBC1 drama series *New Tricks* instead. I, of course, took the job.

I must admit that I have never watched *New Tricks* but I am aware that it is a very popular series which stars (in alphabetical order): Alun Armstrong, James Bolam, Amanda Redman and Dennis Waterman.

I was given a 10am call for *New Tricks*. The location was Potters Fields car park, off Tooley Street in south east

London by the side of Tower bridge. This was set to be one of the famous London landmarks that I would be running across during the *London Marathon* the following Sunday.

There were just eight male extras called to play four architects and four surveyors. Oh, and one female had been called to play a P.A. I was cast as one of the architects and paired with a fellow extra David Horne who was playing a surveyor. It was a glorious day and Tower Bridge looked stunning in the sunlight as we were directed to walk around the dusty car park while Dennis Waterman and Amanda Redman delivered their lines.

It was a really fun 'shoot'. Dave kept singing the *Minder* theme tune (*I Could Be So Good For You*) and eventually I was singing along until we were both laughing too much.

What really had us in hysterics that day was that every time we looked at Dennis Waterman we cracked up as we both started impersonating the *Little Britain* sketch! You may remember the one where David Walliams plays a little version of Dennis Waterman who keeps wanting to 'Write the theme tune and sing the theme tune,' on every acting job he gets! I must add, in case any directors are reading, that as soon as 'action' was called we immediately stopped laughing and behaved as professional extras should!

Following the superb weather we had for the *New Tricks* 'shoot', I watched *GMTV*'s weather forecast on the Thursday morning. I was not too pleased to hear the weather presenter telling viewers that the weather would be taking a turn for the worse with showers predicted and that this would, of course, be bad news for runners in the *London Marathon* that forthcoming Sunday.

On the Friday evening I was relaxing with Suzanne and Melody watching *Hells Kitchen* when the phone started ringing. Callers informed me that they had spotted me in the opening episode of *The Fall and Rise of Reginald Perrin* remake, *Reggie Perrin*. Several texts also came through to my mobile phone from other friends who had seen me in the sitcom.

Another tip for those readers who are budding extras is that you should never tell your family or friends that you are going to be on a particular programme. Usually what happens if you do is that you discover that your appearance has hit the cutting room floor which is very embarrassing!

The scene I had been spotted in during the first episode of *Reggie Perrin* saw me sitting on a train behind Reggie (Martin Clunes) nodding along to the music playing on my *iPod*. I seem to have mastered the art of nodding and no music was required to help enhance my nodding action – indeed, my earphones were not even plugged into my *iPod!*

My nodding has become a standing (or in this case sitting) joke amongst my friends and they look out for it! It's all part of the fun of being a film & TV extra!

Meanwhile, back to the *London Marathon!* On the Friday

I made my way to the *London Marathon Exhibition* at the Excel Centre in London's Docklands area. It was a bit of schlep to get there, but this is where all runners have to register in person and collect their running numbers and timing chip to go on one of their trainers. This then registers your exact starting and finishing time.

On the Saturday I ran 2 miles, my final training before the big day! I relaxed for the rest of the day (or as much as I could!) and went over to friends in the evening. That night I set the alarm for 5.30am but in the event I was up even earlier to have my pre-marathon breakfast. This consisted of Frosted Shreddies, two slices of toast and a banana.

My friend Graham dropped me and his son Jeremy (who was also running) at Edgware Underground Station. We made our way to Charing Cross and by 8 o'clock the station was already heaving with nervous marathon runners!

As I strolled onto Blackheath there was not a cloud in sight. Spotting several runners wearing the *British Heart Foundation* shirts I wished them a good run. I then lined up in Pen 9 for the start of the *29th London Marathon* and at 9am the professional and wheelchair athletes were off, although we just jostled along for about 15 minutes before I actually crossed the starting line at 9.59am.

The warm weather attracted the crowds but quite a few runners suffered in the heat. I actually like running in the sunny weather. A few weeks earlier I had run 12 miles in training on the Costa del Sol with the temperature being far hotter. I had quite a run up to a quaint village called Benahavis, which was rather hilly.

I overtook Katie Price (Jordan) and Peter Andre running together at one point and wished them the best of luck. I cheekily added that I couldn't run with them, as I had to get to Buckingham Palace by 3pm! They seemed to be enjoying the event at that stage, but it took them 7 hours, 11 minutes to cross the finish line. Who could have imagined that in a couple of weeks of me meeting them and taking their photo during the *London Marathon* they would announce to the world on 11th May 2009 that they were splitting up?

I felt I was running a consistent pace and at around 21 miles I saw Nick, the son of my friend Wayne, who was suffering from cramp due to not taking in enough fluid during the race. I checked my time and realised that I had a chance of beating my 2004 time of 4 hours 43 minutes and 15 seconds. Despite my legs really aching at this stage, I tried to run as fast as I could. The crowd spurred me on and as I pushed myself along Birdcage Walk towards Buckingham Palace my eyes welled up with emotion. A massive sign which stated that there were just 385 yards to go signalled that I was almost there. I ran by Buckingham Palace and could see the finishing line in sight. Pushing myself as hard as I physically could I crossed the line with a time of 4 hours 39 minutes and 17 seconds! At the age of 54 I had run the fastest of my four *London Marathon's*. I was exhausted but exhilarated at the same time.

Suzanne, Melody and my friend Simone then met me at the top of St James Park. It was an amazing day.

For those of you reading who like facts and figures, here are those for the *2009 London Marathon:*

- 155,245 people applied to run, the highest ever
- 36,156 runners registered to start
- 35,747 runners actually started
- 35,306 runners finished
- 441 runners did not finish
- Paul Wilder came in 15,681 with a personal best time of 4 hours 39 minutes and 17 seconds

Paul B: So, with Paul having crossed the finishing line during his various entries in the London Marathon – *and now for this book – I then asked him what his hopes and plans are for the future:*

Paul W: Well, I certainly hope that I have many more years left before I cross the ultimate finishing line! During this time I hope that life will bring me further fun challenges and the chance to spend even more quality time with my family.

I hope this book has inspired you, the reader, to consider having a go at some of the realistic ambitions and goals you hold. You never know what you are capable of achieving until you try!

Oh yes, and as for my on-going quest for TV fame? It continues …

THE QUEST CONTINUES

Postscript

In May 2009, Suzanne and I decided to have a few days break in Spain. This would also be an ideal opportunity for me to read through the second draft of the manuscript of this book that Paul Burton had sent me.

After a couple of hours of reading by the pool, I decided to lie back on my sun bed and listen to some music. I had tuned some local English speaking radio stations into my *Nokia 6300* mobile. Even while abroad, I like to flick through stations like *Spectrum 105.5 FM, Wave 96.0 FM* and *The Beat 106.0 FM,* to name just a few.

While listening to one of the stations a DJ mentioned celebrity chef Jean-Christophe Novelli and his 'Tasting Experiences'. I mentioned this to Suzanne and suggested it might be something that both she and our friends Yvonne and Graham, who are 'foodies', would enjoy. Suzanne proposed that we pop into the Locrimar Hotel where Novelli had recently opened a new restaurant to find out what it was all about. The hotel was not too far from where we were staying.

Now having mentioned previously I am a plain food eater, a food tasting session was not high on my list of things to do while on holiday. However, not being averse to meeting a celebrity I ran along with the idea!

We popped into Novelli's restaurant and an English-speaking member of staff explained that the 'Novelli Tasting Experience' would cost 250 euros per person. As we were discussing the cost (there was no way we would be going to the tasting!), the man himself appeared. He very politely ushered us out of the restaurant and into the bar area to look at the menu. I then noticed a sign referring to dress code in the restaurant. I was inappropriately dressed in shorts and T-shirt!

Meanwhile, Suzanne and Yvonne were discussing how good-looking Jean-Christophe was together with his sexy French accent. I had a chat to his brother Anthony Novelli who was the Maitre'd. I explained that we would not be attending the tasting experience, but would phone and book a table in the restaurant later in the week.

That night we went from the sublime to the ridiculous eating at Peggotty's, arguably the best fish and chips on the Costa del Sol. As we tucked in to our enormous portions of cod and chips we discussed dining at Novelli's. It was a no-brainer for the girls, they wanted to go back to see Jean-Christophe. I telephoned to book a table but the card that Anthony had given me had the incorrect number.

So after our incredibly filling fish and chips we drove the short distance to the Locrimar Hotel to personally book a table. Once again Jean-Christophe was there in person. Now having perused the menu that included a starter of:

Cappuccino style soup
Roasted honey, pumpkin and sand carrot veloute soup garnished with garrene rabbit rillette, local prunes topped with toasted pumpkin seeds and parmesan froth.

A main course of:

Burgos lamb
Marinated with wild mountain herbs and served pink, herb crust, manzanilla olive mash, rioja salsify, liquorice cream.

Having read the whole menu I decided to ask the man himself if he could cater for a plain fussy eater like me. 'Is it ok to have a plain steak and pomme frites?' I asked.

Having watched Marco Pierre White on Hell's Kitchen, I wondered if I would be thrown out of the restaurant for daring to ask for a 'well done' steak! I was delighted that Jean-Christophe replied: 'Nussing is a problem.'

On Sunday 24th May 2009 some other friends joined us at Novelli's and I tucked into some plain water melon as a starter followed by a well done sirloin steak with six hand cut chips stacked in a 'jenga' formation.

I could quite easily have skipped the starters and main course and gone straight for dessert, which I have to say was sensational. Steering away from the very tempting Chocolate Fondant, my choice was:

Apple tarte tatin 'Jean-Christophe Novelli'
Flavoured with calvados, vanilla bourbon ice cream
(*Please allow 20 minutes*)

I have to say, it was well worth the wait!

The restaurant was not full and Jean-Christophe was being the perfect host, spending time with each and every person there. At around 11:15pm our host came over to our table to chat to us all. Our wives were particularly entranced by his presence.

Never one to miss an opportunity, I told Jean-Christophe about my book and my quest for TV fame and how I had appeared on TV shows like *Big Brother's Big Mouth* and *I'm a Celeb*.

Jean-Christophe said: 'Yes I know, I recognise you from the TV!' Quick as a flash he continued: 'Sank you for the 50 euros you slipped me at the bar to say zat.' Of course this was a genuinely funny moment. He was an absolute charmer and when I asked him if he would write a good luck message on my manuscript, he said: 'Of course.' He wrote:

My profound Best Wishes
To your successful future!
If a kiss won't do, the cooking will!
Well done
A Bientot!
Jean x
24-05-09 Spain!

That, to me seems like a good note to end this book on. So may I take this opportunity to thank you for reading: *Paul Wilder: My Quest for TV Fame*.

Game Show and Quiz Show Credits

1989
Every Second Counts

1990
All Clued Up

Chain Letters

Everybody's Equal

Keynotes

Laughlines

The Mike Smith Show

Sale of the Century

Takeover Bid (rehearsals)

Wife of the Week

1991
Fast Friends

The James Whale Radio Show

Lucky Ladders

2000
Blankety Blank (standby contestant)

It's Anybody's Guess

The National Lottery Jet Set (standby contestant)

Wheel of Fortune

2001
Greed

King of the Castle

The Biggest Game in Town

The People Versus

2002
Test the Nation

The Weakest Link

Wipeout

2003
Celebrity Addicts

GASH

Stars Reunited

2004
I'm the Answer

Chat and Discussion Show Credits

1991
Tonight with Jonathan Ross

2007
Big Brother's Big Mouth

Celebrity Big Brother's Big Mouth

Get Your Act Together – The Showdown

I'm a Celebrity Get Me Out of Here...Now!

2008
Big Brother documentary (for Keshet TV)

Big Brother's Big Mouth

Celebrity Hijack – Big Brother's Big Mouth

I'm A Celebrity Get Me Out of Here...Now!

The TV Show

2009
Big Brother's Big Mouth

Celebrity Big Brother's Big Mouth

TNT Show

Supporting Artist Credits

2006
EastEnders

Run, Fatboy, Run

The Bill

The Bourne Ultimatum

2007
Ashes to Ashes

Cape Wrath

EastEnders

He Kills Coppers

Holby Blue

Holby City

Hotel Babylon

Miss Pettigrew Lives for a Day

PC World (commercial)

The Bill

The Candidate

Transmanche Ferries (commercial)

2008
After You've Gone

Caught in a Trap

Demons (The Last Van Helsing)

Harley Street

Hells Pavement

Holby City

Ikea (commercial)

JML – Conductor's Choice Classics (commercial)

Law and Order UK

Mr Eleven

Nike (commercial)

Reggie Perrin

Secret Diary of a Call Girl

The Bill

The Sunday Night Project

2009
Coming of Age

Day of the Triffids

Law and Order UK

New Tricks

Orange Wednesday (commercial)

Spooks

The Bill

The Thick of It

ORDER FORM

You can order further copies of this book from
SMP Publishers either online at:
www.smppublishers.co.uk
or by using this order form.

DELIVERY: UK – £2.00, Europe – £3.95,
Worldwide – £6.95 p&p (may change) per book.

To order further copies of
Paul Wilder: My Quest for TV Fame,
please send a copy of this form to:

> SMP Publishers
> Devonshire House
> Manor Way
> Borehamwood
> Hertfordshire
> WD6 1QQ

Please send me _____ copies @ £7.99 each of:
Paul Wilder: My Quest for TV Fame

I enclose a UK bank cheque or postal order, payable to:
SMP Publishers for: £_____

Name: _____

Address: _____

_____

_____ Postcode: _____

Email: _____

Tick here if you wish to be added to our mailing list: ☐

Please allow 28 days for delivery. Do not send cash through the post.
Offer subject to availability. Please note: we do not share customer
details with any third parties.